KU-760-464

MODERN AMERICAN
FIGHTING KNIVES

MODERN AMERICAN FIGHTING KNIVES

By Robert S. McKay

DISCLAIMER

Please note that the publisher of this instructional book is NOT RESPONSIBLE in any manner whatsoever for any injury which may occur by reading and/or following the instructions herein.

It is essential that before following any of the activities, physical or otherwise, herein described, the reader or readers should first consult his or her physician for advice on whether or not the reader or readers should embark on the physical activity described herein. Since the physical activities described herein may be too sophisticated in nature, it is essential that a physician be consulted.

Unique Publications
4201 Vanowen Place
Burbank, CA 91505

ISBN: 0-86568-086-8
Library of Congress Catalog Number: 86-51211

© 1987 by Unique Publications. All rights reserved.
Published 1987. Printed in the United States of America.

Designer: Danilo J. Silverio
Editor: Russell Maynard
Cover Photo: Barrett Stinson

Basic Dagger Design

SPEAR POINT

SHARPENED EDGES

CHOIL

CROSS GUARD

SYMMETRICAL, FOIL-SHAPED HANDLE OR HILT

POMMEL

Basic Bowie Design

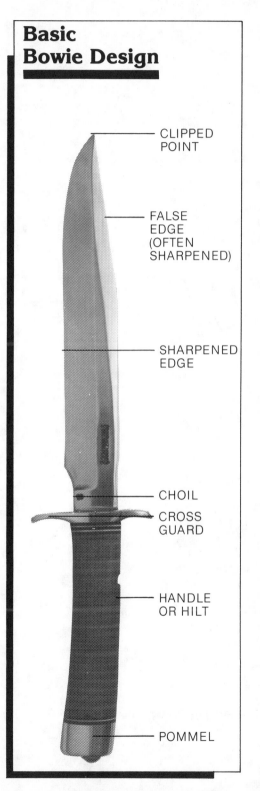

CLIPPED POINT

FALSE EDGE (OFTEN SHARPENED)

SHARPENED EDGE

CHOIL

CROSS GUARD

HANDLE OR HILT

POMMEL

Table of Contents

INTRODUCTION: Separating Myth From Reality

Of all the weapons currently available for civilian self-defense, none is a misunderstood as the fighting knife. Many of today's books and popular films depict knife combat in a TOTALLY unrealistic manner. This has led to the perpetuation of various myths of knife fighting, most of which will probably get you KILLED in an actual self-defense confrontation.

One of the goals of this book is to expose these myths. Out on the streets, it's sometimes more important to know what NOT to do, than what TO do. Avoiding the pitfalls posed by knife fighting mythology may very well save your life!

As the title suggests, this is a book totally devoted to AMERICAN fighting knives and combat methods. This is not intended as a "put down" of the Oriental martial arts, which deserve full merit and respect. However, no one book can hope to cover all the intricacies of knife fighting without being overly simplistic. Many have tried, and most have failed. For this reason, I have limited the scope of this book to American knife fighting techniques and blade designs without attempting to compare or contrast them with other combat systems or knife designs. There are several other fine books on Asian systems of knife fighting available today. I recommend them heartily to the interested reader.

Many books on knife fighting assume that the reader is familiar with the unique nomenclature of blade design. Since it is my opinion that HOW YOU USE a knife is more relevant than what it's made of or how it's designed, the use of technical terms has been kept to a minimum. Line drawings of basic dagger and Bowie designs, with the parts labeled, have been included for the reader's convenience.

In conclusion, I would like to dedicate this book to those in the field of close-combat whose respect and gracious assistance I could not have done without in compiling this work: Colonel Rex Applegate (USA-Ret.) the living "Dean" of American close-quarter combat; Bradley J. Steiner, my good friend and founder of the Combato System; Jesse Glover and Jeff "J.T." Thompson, who introduced me to non-classical gung-fu; and to Lin Steiner, Todd Ackley, and Mike Franz for their assistance as models and devotion as students of the combat arts.

PART ONE
The Evolution of American Fighting Knives

The development of firearms forever changed the role of edge weapons in combat. Rifles replaced swords, spears and halberts on the battlefield, and for personal defense, the pistol became the preferred armament. In 18th Century America, the men who explored, conquered and "civilized" this country were the first to create and refine the concept of a knife that would serve as a back-up defensive weapon to their firearms.

From the pioneers and mountain men, we inherited the utility/fighter; a knife short and light enough to carry across the Great Divide, yet with enough strength and heft to build a cabin or split the skull of any wild man or animal who got past their rifles. It was the river boat gamblers and gold town dandies who gave us the concealable knife, a hole card discreetly tucked under a coat in case their pocket pistol couldn't settle a disagreement between gentlemen. From Bowies to switchblades, push-daggers to trench knives, the evolution of the modern fighting knife has become an American institution.

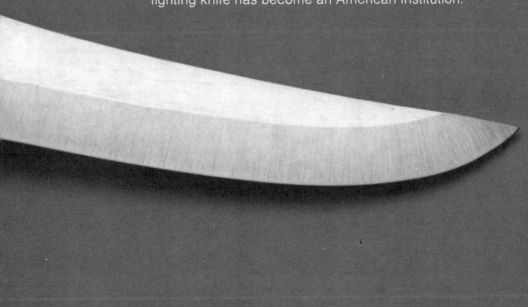

Early History of Fighting Blades

Although what we now term a "knife" was not really developed until mankind learned to use metals, our Stone Age ancestors were quite adept with bladed and pointed weapons flaked from flint, obsidian, quartz and other types of fine-grained rock. During the Stone Age, cutting weapons were not incorporated with stabbing weapons due to the brittleness of the stone itself; a wafer-thin piece of flint was as sharp as a razor for slicing, but too brittle to be used as a thrusting point. Conversely, thrusting spear points were stout and had no blades for cutting.

By about 7000 BC, the Mesopotamians were fashioning knives from copper, and by 3500 BC, the Egyptians were

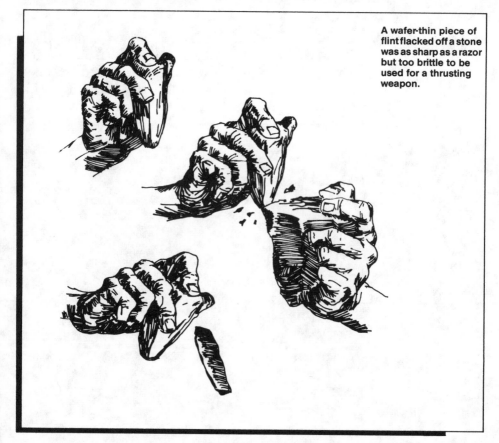

A wafer-thin piece of flint flacked off a stone was as sharp as a razor but too brittle to be used for a thrusting weapon.

beginning to utilize blades as military weapons. The Sumerians were making bronze knives by 2500 BC, and by 1500 BC, the Philistines were fashioning swords from iron. Because metals like iron could be "worked," it was possible to incorporate cutting and stabbing functions into the same weapon; the knife.

Up until the advent of firearms, the sword was the frontline weapon in most of the world. Knives were only used as back-ups, or to finish off downed opponents by thrusting through their heavy armor. When firearms made armor obsolete, swords began to shrink in size and weight and no longer required both of a fighter's hands to wield.

By the 15th Century, the rapier — a straight, double-edged sword with a narrow blade and point — had replaced the heavy broadswords of old. Combatants faced each other with the rapier forward, rear hand clutching a dagger for warding off the opposing blade or for finishing off the antagonist if grappling ensued. In a 1604 work by the fencing master Agrippa, the dagger is mentioned as a supplement to the rapier, more suited to "sticking frogs" than for gentlemanly combat.

For the next two hundred years, European swords tended to become stronger and lighter. Soon, blocking and parrying was done exclusively with the sword, and the use of a dagger

The Italian Guards with the Sword & Dagger.
Publish'd as the Act directs Aug.ᵗ 1783

in the rear hand fell into disuse. Also, as blades continued to get lighter and thinner, they lost the weight needed for effective slashing. Sword fighting, or "foil fencing," came to rely almost exclusively on the stabbing thrust, featuring the use of either the foil or epee. Because fencers now relied exclusively on the strong hand to hold the sword, they could turn sideways to limit the target presented to any enemy.

By the late 17th Century, fencing had become a gentleman's art and a favorite method of settling disagreements through recourse to duelling. Schools for fencing instruction — called *salles d' armes* — sprang up across Europe, and each nation had its own fencing champions. At these schools, the well-to-do learned to defend both their "persons and their honor from attack or insult."

Although firearms were available during these periods, they were expensive and difficult to use. Matchlock and flintlock pistols were all single shot, bulky, slow to load, and prone to malfunction; even if you got off a shot, you'd have to rely on your sword if you missed or were facing multiple foes. While the military value of firearms was well-established by 1800, the sword continued to be the preferred civilian weapon throughout most of Europe.

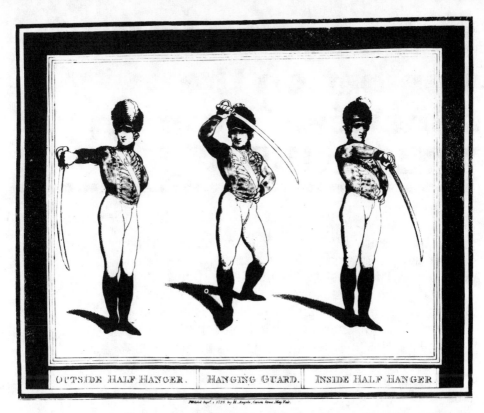

OUTSIDE HALF HANGER. | HANGING GUARD. | INSIDE HALF HANGER.

Published Aug.t 1 1799 by H. Angelo, Curzon Street May Fair.

Two types of slashing swords also evolved from the rapier; the saber, primarily used by cavalry, and the cutlass, a short sword used by sailors during boardings. More stout than the foil, sabers usually featured a curved, sharpened bottom edge designed for slashing as well as a relatively narrow point for thrusting. Cutlasses were generally shorter, with broader blades and points, much like a machete. Both featured large handguards or "bells" for warding off an opponent's blade and to protect the user's hand. In battle, these slashing swords were more practical than foils or the epee because fighting occurred en masse, not face-to-face, one-on-one, as in duels. At extremely close quarters, a sailor or cavalryman could slash, but could seldom execute a solid thrust, ESPECIALLY from horseback or in a confined space like a ship's cabin.

Today, these weapons are still found in the two basic types of sport fencing; foil and saber style. And by 1810, both styles were being taught at *salles d' armes* in New Orleans, St. Louis and New York. Most of these schools also offered pistol instruction as well. Beginning about 1830, however, the sword began to be replaced by that "most-American" of all fighting blades, the Bowie knife.

THE BOWIE DESIGN: Combat on the American Frontier, 1827-1865

During the early 1800s, the single-shot pistol and knife were replacing the sword as the weapons of choice among American civilians, just as the musket and bayonet replaced the pike for the infantry soldier. In 1827, Rezin P. Bowie traveled from his home in Kentucky to seek medical attention in Philadelphia. While there, he submitted a hunting knife design, based on that of a Spanish dagger, to a master bladesmith named Henry Shively. The knifemaker modified the design somewhat himself — adding a cross guard, shortening the blade to 9 inches, and providing a "clip point" atop the blade that was not initially sharpened. Rezin Bowie was most pleased with what turned out to be the very first "Bowie Knife."

After hearing that his brother had become involved in some difficulties with a man named Norris Wright, Rezin gave his single-edged knife to James Bowie for personal protection. On his way to Texas in 1828, it's alleged that Jim Bowie showed the blade to a knifemaker in Arkansas named James Black, who suggested that Bowie sharpen the false edge for slashing in both directions and for better stabbing penetration. Few substantial improvements have been made to the basic Bowie design since then.

After his heroic death at the Alamo in 1836, the exploits of Jim Bowie and his famous fighting knife made it the new weapon of choice (along with the pistol) on the American frontier. During the Vidalia Sandbar Fight (some skeptical historians refer to it as a brawl), Bowie allegedly killed his nemesis Norris Wright with the knife after receiving two pistol wounds and a stab from a sword cane. In 1829, Bowie is reported to have fought a Natchez gambler named Sturdivant, who had cheated Bowie in a card game. Supposedly their weak-side wrists were tied together for

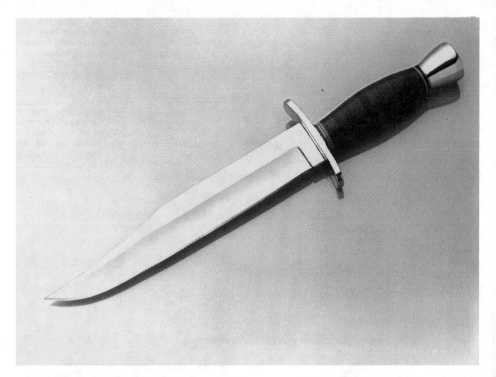

A modern, 10" Bowie fighter from Al Mar knives.

a duel; when Sturdivant attacked, Bowie parried and cut his opponent's knife arm, disarming him, but magnanimously allowed him to live. Or so the story goes.

Sturdivant, however, wouldn't let bygones be bygones. He hired three thugs to ambush Bowie on his return trip to Texas. As one assassin rushed from the brush and grabbed his horse's bridle, Bowie slashed right through his throat, almost severing the head. After being stabbed in the thigh, Bowie fell from his horse but chased down one of the other two attackers and disemboweled him. Catching up to the last fleeing hit man, Bowie allegedly split his skull open with his heavy blade.

Whether the stories concerning Bowie's exploits are fact or fiction, he became the epitome of the American knife fighter in the early 1800's. The Bowie-type knife suddenly became standard gear for every man west of the Appalachians. As one historian noted, "The day of the civilian sword had passed. Instead the well-equipped gentleman carried a pistol in his pocket and a knife beneath his coattails."

From 1830 until after the Civil War, the Bowie knife and pistol remained the front-line weapons in the American West. At the various *salles d' armes* in New Orleans

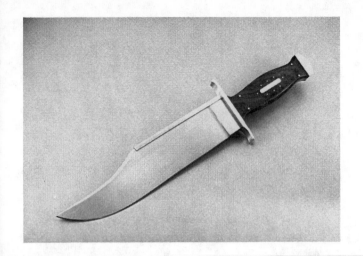

The original Bowies of the 1830's were large, heavy knives, but much less ornate than this custom piece by Pat Crawford (left).

By 1870, the handgun had replaced the bowie as the frontline defensive weapon, which is still the case today (Knife below by Pat Crawford).

and along the Mississippi River, instruction was offered in saber fencing with the Bowie knife. Hundreds of different Bowie knife designs were offered, the best models being imported from Sheffield, England. During the Civil War itself, the Bowie was a favorite weapon of many Confederate soldiers, due to the lack of firearms and ammunition throughout the South.

After 1865, the fighting knife virtually disappeared from the self-defense scene, replaced by the Colt revolver, Winchester repeating rifle and other innovations in firearm technology. Just as the rifle replaced the musket on the battlefield, so too did the revolver replace the Bowie knife for civilian self-defense.

Evaluating The Bowie Design

In any discussion relating to the use of Bowie-type knives for self-defense, it's important to realize that the America of 1828 is not the America of today, and that most modern Bowie knives are not facsimiles of the original weapon used by their namesake at the Vidalia Sandbar. Many well-known knife experts consider the Bowie design to be the ultimate in fighting knives. Frankly, it's hard to understand why. Without meaning any disrespect, I'd suggest that many experts have simply mistaken romantic legends for mundane reality.

The fact is, the original early Bowie of the 1800's was more of a shortened saber than a knife. With broad, heavy blades measuring anywhere from 9 to 23 inches in length, the Bowie was indeed capable of severing heads or lopping off hands. But this is due not so much to the DESIGN of the knife as to the SIZE of it; you can buy a machete at most hardware stores that will accomplish the same result. On the American Frontier of 1828, a man didn't have to worry about practical carry or concealment of a Bowie knife that was over 15 inches long and weighed more than a Colt .45 auto. It was also intended for uses other than fighting; skinning game, cutting and splitting wood, digging and a variety of other survival applications.

That was then, and this is now. In the modern world, it's impractical — and often ILLEGAL — to carry such knives either in full view or concealed beneath clothing.

Many modern blade designers have tried to overcome this problem by making their Bowie-type knives shorter and lighter, but this is like robbing Peter to pay Paul; weight and size are — or were — the most important features of the old fighting Bowie. Without them, the Bowie is somewhat inferior to the basic fighting dagger for a number of reasons.

To begin with, the top of the traditional Bowie blade does not provide an edged cutting surface along its entire length. This, I feel, needlessly limits the knife's slashing potential. Even if the short, concave-bevelled area behind the clipped point is sharpened (refered to as a "false edge"), the remaining portion of the blade top is virtually useless. In recognition of this weakness, some designers have extended a sharpened upper edge almost all the way back to the crossguard (called a "straight clip point), which allows more versatility for slashing and facilitates better stabbing penetration. In so doing, what they've actually done is to modify the Bowie into a variation of a symmetrical fighting dagger.

Another drawback of the basic Bowie is the extended, often elaborate crossguards, reminiscent of those used on the daggers of the Middle Ages. These crossguards were used not only to protect the wielder's hand, but to catch and immobilize an opponent's sword blade. While this was marginally feasible against a sword, it is doubtful that many knife fights — even in Jim Bowie's day — involved combatants locking knives together at the crossguards. It is absolutely ABSURD to attempt such intricate maneuvers against today's shorter knives, especially when wielded by criminal attackers who are looking to take a victim by surprise, not engage in gentlemanly duels. While a moderate crossguard is needed to keep your hand from sliding onto the blade, the extended guards found on most Bowie knives are inclined to become tangled in your clothing as you try to draw them for action. This is simply another carryover from fencing that has no place in modern knife fighting.

Orientation of the blade is another problem with the Bowie. Since its edges are not symmetrical, it's quite possible to grip the knife upside-down by accident, especially in the dark where most knife fights tend to occur. For thrusting purposes this isn't much of a problem, but if you're carrying a Bowie with a short false edge, you may

Locking crossguards during a knife fight isn't likely in the modern world, although this locking lug design (page 14) from Phill Hartsfield could snap an opponent's blade during such a confrontation.

Hartsfield incorporates this unique design into many of his knives, including this "Mountain Man Combat/Camp" knife.

His latest design, a collector's Bowie, has an oval-shaped guard, and the handle is formed for a "Hammer fist" grip.

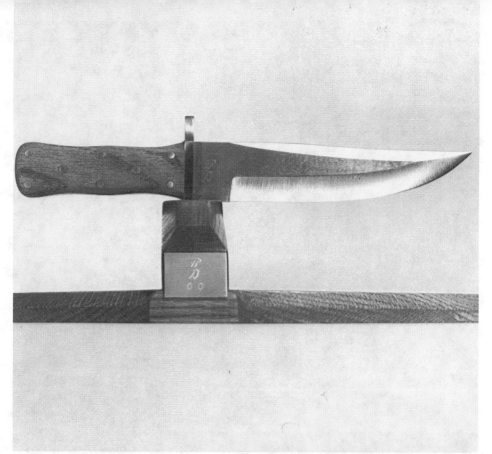

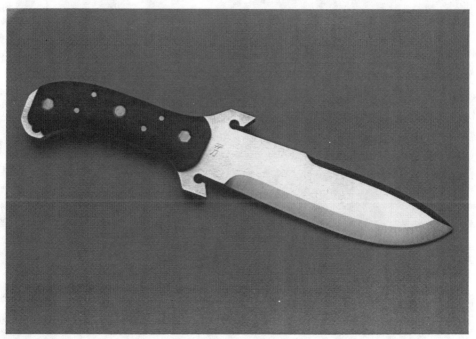

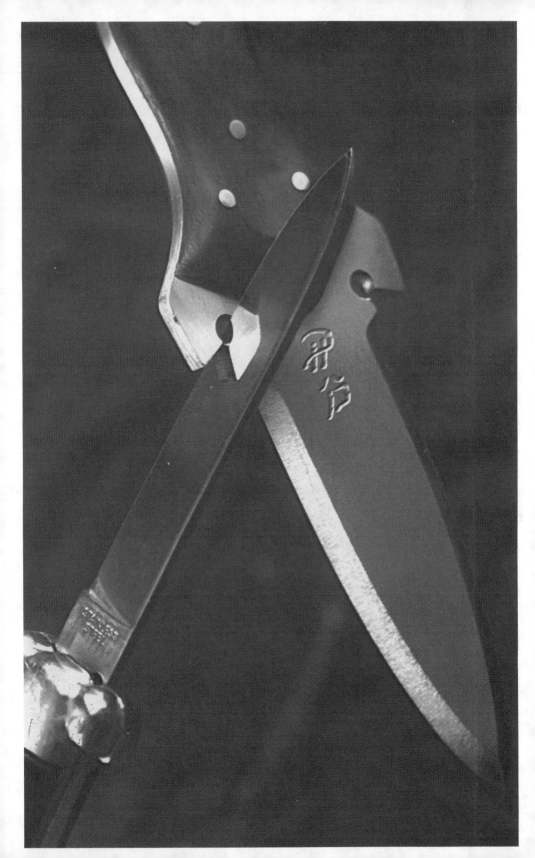

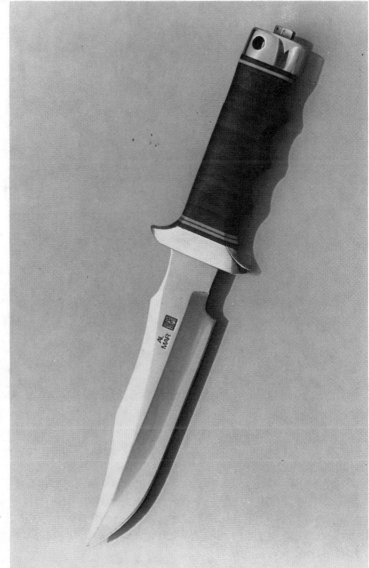

The 12" long Indian Bowie (top) by Robert Parrish is ideal for concealed carry; no crossguard to snag on clothing, a sharpened straight top edge and thumb grooves on top for proper orientation of the blade.

Orientation of the Bowie blade can be crucial. This new SF-SOG design by Al Mar features a finger-grooved handle, which should prevent an incorrect grip.

Arnold Schwarzenneger demonstrates the hammer grip with his Skorpion Survival Bowie made by Jack Crain for the movie, "Commando".

find yourself slashing with the wrong part of the blade. Again, some designers have overcome this problem with longer false edges and specialized handles, thus properly orienting the blade to grip.

One criticism of the Bowie I personally feel lacks substance concerns the clipped point and the use of the "hammer grip" (covered in detail in Part II) for thrusting. Most proponents of knife "fencing" swear by the "saber grip." They consider the hammer grip suitable only for "amateurs," and lament the fact that the upturned, clipped point of the Bowie is best used for thrusting upward with the hammer grip. When one considers how many people Jim Bowie is alleged to have disembowelled with just such a grip, it is difficult to follow what these people are complaining about. The hammer grip is far stronger, and in some ways, more versatile than the saber grip preferred by many experts. It is especially valuable when stabbing with a thick-bladed Bowie, since the large blade requires a great deal of power for deep penetration. So-called "amateurs" using the hammer grip kill thousands of people in the U.S. every year. We will cover this topic, a bit later and in more detail, in Chapter Eight.

The Bowie-Style Survival Knife

Although the Bowie is not TECHNICALLY the best choice for a PURE fighting knife, it does serve quite well as a multipurpose survival knife. The need for such a tool arose initially during WWI and became even more noticeable in WWII when troops found themselves in need of a knife for opening cans, cutting brush, sharpening tent pegs AND dispatching enemy sentries in the dead of night.

During WWI, the American Mark I trench knife, essentially a dagger blade with a knuckle bow for a handle, proved to be inadequate and very unpopular among the troops. The thin symmetrical blade often broke at the tang when used for prying, and the points were so weak, they often snapped off when used to open cans.

In WWII, the need for a durable survival knife became even more apparent, particularly in Asian jungles where soldiers, downed pilots and clandestine units often were forced to live off the land for weeks at a time. With the development of light, full-auto machine guns, and the decline of close-quarter trench warfare, the knife became more valuable as a tool and was used less and less as a weapon in WWII.

For survival purposes, the Bowie is far preferable to the dagger. With its broad, clipped-point blade, it can be used for prying or punching through mangled metal without fear of breakage. Since its blade thickness is greater than that of most daggers, and generally tapers from top

One of the earliest Bowie-type survival knives used during WWII was the Kabar (opposite page), officially adopted by the U.S. Marine Corps for use in the Pacific. The blade is parkerized to reduce glare and prevent rust. One of the most famous survival knives is this one (right) from Jimmy Lile, used by Sylvester Stallone in the movie "First Blood". It illustrates some of the most popular of today's survival knife features; saw teeth, a wrapped cylindrical handle, and a removable butt cap and hollow handle for storing matches, fishing line or even a compass.

A slightly-modified version (below) was made especially for the sequel "Rambo".

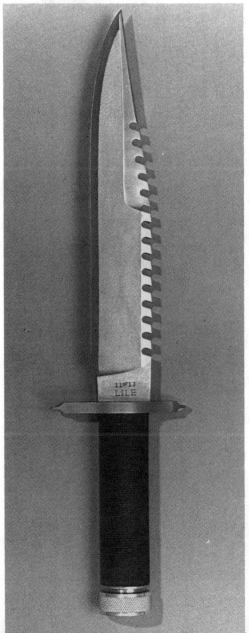

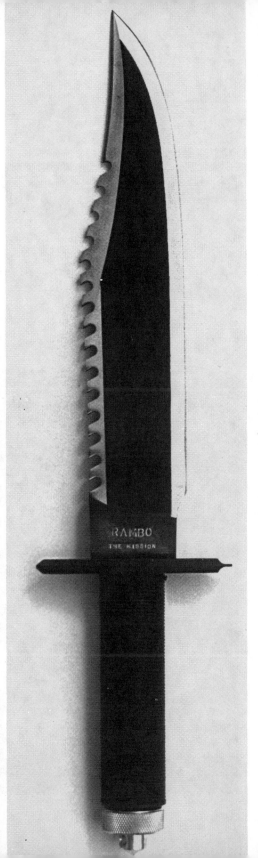

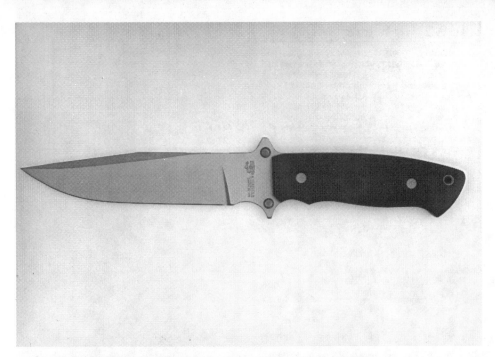

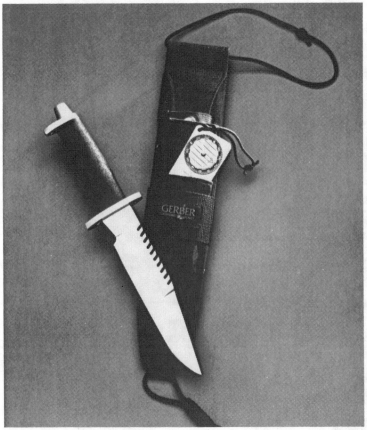

This "Fieldmaster" survival knife by Bob Terzuola (above) is a heavy knife which can serve a variety of applications.

The BMF survival knife from Gerber (left) comes with its own hone and compass in a Cordura sheath. This knife is also available without the saw teeth. The Buckmaster (opposite) features a water and air tight hollow handle with saw teeth for cutting wood, rope and even metal.

The Buckmaster LT (at
right of Buckmaster
on opposite page)
features the same
blade but with a
skeletonized handle
coated in
thermoplastic.

The Woodsmate and
Fieldmate with Kraton
handles (above) are
versatile Bowie
designs for hunting or
survival uses.

A solid tang survival blade (left) fashioned by Pat Crawford from tool steel, blued for a non-glare protective finish.

Some of the most heavy duty hollow-handle survival knives are made by Steve Allen of Running River Supply. His basic Bowie survivor (below) as available with or without saw teeth and engraving.

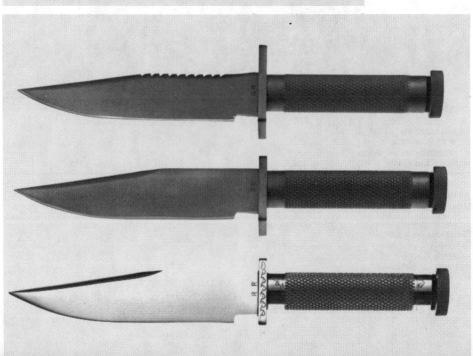

Allen's knife (right) comes with a sturdy sheath, a compass mounted in the butt cap and a sharpening stone.

The "Wilderness Edge" from Tekna (below) features a full-tang skeletal blade with an exposed blade sheath. The plastic handle contains a waterproof flashlight, while the sheath includes a compass, fire starter, animal snare, signal mirror, sharpener and even a collapsible fishing reel.

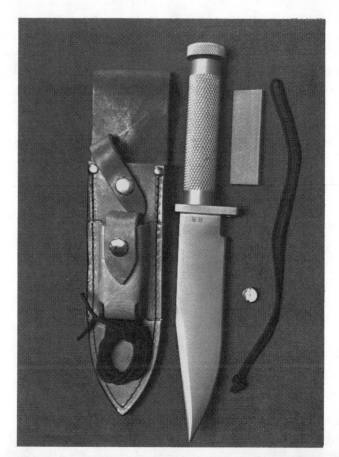

to bottom, there is little chance that the point will snap off when chopping, prying or piercing with it.

Most of today's best survival knives are still based on a modified Bowie design, with some exceptions like the Gerber Mark II. Some feature saw teeth for cutting wood, and hollow handles for storing matches, fishing lines or even money.

SUMMATION:
The Bowie in
Civilian Self-Defense

Let me conclude by saying, all-in-all, the Bowie is probably the BEST all-around survival design ever conceived. It's also an excellent fighting knife — but not technically the BEST TYPE of PURE fighting knife available for civilian self-defense. On the streets of New York or Chicago, you shouldn't need to open tin cans, saw through saplings or start a fire with matches concealed in the hollow handle. What you should have is a knife designed strictly for combat, and the best possible design for that is the fighting dagger.

Two knives from Crain. The survival Bowie has all the features that are currently popular, but for urban survival, the short semi-dagger above it is more practical.

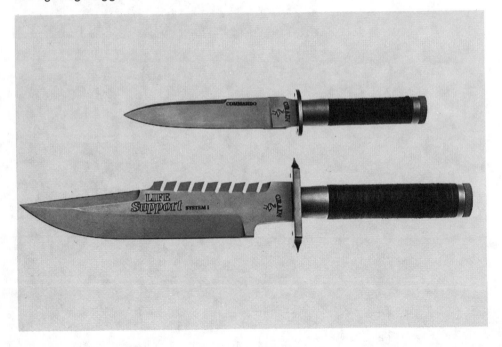

THE DAGGER DESIGN: From Trench to Commando Knives, 1917-1945

Although the dagger has been around for centuries, it did not really begin to compete with the Bowie as a favored American fighting blade until after WWI. As a survival or hunting knife, the dagger leaves much to be desired. But for slashing and thrusting—the essentials of knife fighting — the dagger is hard to match.

During WWI, the U.S. introduced the Mark I trench knife to serve as both a survival tool and weapon for close-in trench combat. It failed miserably in both capacities. The thin, double-edged blade was too fragile for prying and general use, while the knuckle-bow handle made it difficult to carry and hard to wield in a fight.

At the outbreak of WWII, another legendary fighting blade was introduced to Allied troops; the Fairbairn-Sykes Fighting Knife. Designed by Capt. W.E. Fairbairn and Capt. Eric Anthony Sykes of Shanghai fame (see Chapter 6), the Fairbairn-Sykes was initially issued to the British Commandoes and other elite Allied forces, including the U.S. Marines and clandestine operatives of the Office of Strategic Services — now known as the Central Intelligence Agency.

The Fairbairn-Sykes was immensely popular with Allied troops during the war, over 200,000 of them were issued, and it was this very popularity that eventually contributed to its downfall. Although the very first blades manufactured in England were excellent fighting weapons, shortages of material and an increasing demand soon led to production shortcuts that drastically lowered the quality of the knife. Hastily-produced blades were often overly brittle causing breakage at the tang and point. Another problem to arise involved the brass foil-shaped handle, which was originally specified for the Fairbairn-Sykes.

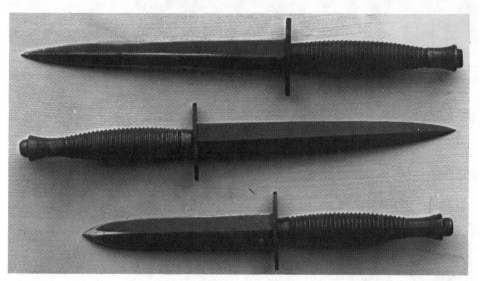

The Fairbairn-Sykes Commando knife was widely used during WWII by clandestine agents behind enemy lines. The two at top are original WWII versions from Sheffield, England, while the re-pointed shorty is an inferior copy with a snapped off point.

Since brass was scarce during the war, various manufacturers began using wood, leather, wound hemp, aluminum and other substitutes for the handle. This profoundly changed the balance of the original design, and in some cases, increased its overall weight twofold.

Many of today's critics — particularly those from the "fencing" school — have dismissed the Fairbairn-Sykes as a serious fighting knife without considering Fairbairn's theory of application. While there certainly were plenty of flaws in the production versions of the knife, Fairbairn and his counterpart at the O.S.S., Col. Rex Applegate, were well aware of them by 1943. We will examine these shortcomings, but first, let's look at the knife's positive attributes.

One of the most valuable innovations provided by the Fairbairn-Sykes was a sheath designed for concealment and a fast draw. The metal-tipped sheath included leather tabs for sewing into pants pockets, up coat sleeves or into boot tops. The knife was also retained by a small elastic loop, which facilitated a fast release from almost any carry position.

This is a subject often ignored by the knife's critics who tend to focus their attention exclusively on the knife itself. Fairbairn and Sykes did not design their knife for one-on-one, face-to-face duelling. The commandoes and special operatives, for whom the knife was intended, were almost always fighting behind enemy lines and had to depend on the knife for quick, surprise kills. Many were spies and saboteurs who had to conceal their weapons

Unlike survival knives, the F-S was designed for quick kills, often from behind in an offensive manner.

from enemy occupiers. When the knife did come into play, it was used for sentry removal from behind or for quick, THRUSTING kills against an enemy armed with rifle, machine gun or pistol — NOT AGAINST opponents armed with knives. Some of the criticisms of the blade — that its crossguard isn't long enough for catching other blades and its tip may stick during a slash — are, to put it bluntly, patently absurd when you consider the knife's intended function.

During a recent conversation with Col. Rex Applegate of the OSS, he explained Fairbairn's approach to the use of the knife very clearly. "Whenever a new civilian or military trainee arrived at Area B (the Close Combat Section of the OSS training facility at Camp David, Maryland), Fairbairn would engage him in innocent conversation at arm's length. Once Fairbairn felt his subject to be off-guard, he would reach casually into the front pocket of his British battle dress, and with lightning speed, draw his knife and put it to the throat of the unsuspecting trainee."

In this way, Applegate pointed out, the trainees were taught that close combat with the knife depended more on preparation, surprise, cunning and ruthlessness; NOT FENCING TECHNIQUES. No doubt, most of Fairbairn's "marks" became instant believers in this doctrine!

POST WAR FIGHTING DAGGERS: Evolution of the Fairbairn-Sykes

As a thrusting, quick-kill knife, the original Fairbairn-Sykes was a fine weapon for the commando or OSS operative. But it was too fragile to be used as a multi-purpose survival tool for the soldier, and there were other problems that prevented it from being a good slashing blade. Fairbairn himself realized that there were three major weaknesses in the original Fairbairn-Sykes design:

1) The narrow, thick, stiletto-like blade did not provide the type of edge needed for effective slashing.

2) Reports from operatives in the field indicated that the blade was too weak at the tip and tang, often breaking at these points.

3) The round, foil-type handle tended to slip in a sweaty

This version of the Applegate-Fairbairn fighter (opposite page) will soon be available from Al Mar knives. Many experts consider it to be the ultimate fighting knife design.

Top, two legendary fighting knife designs –the Randall #2 fighting "stilletto" and #1"fighting Bowie" from Randall-Made knives. Note that this Bowie has a dagger-width blade and a lengthened, bevelled sharp edge for improved slashing. Foil-like handle of the #1 is also curved for proper blade orientation when drawing.

The modern Mark I and Mark II survival knives (right) from Gerber feature solid aluminum alloy handles and sturdy double-edged blades of tool steel. Sheaths are made of water-repellant Cordura with quick release thumb snaps.

palm, making it difficult to draw the knife with the blade properly oriented.

In 1943, Fairbairn and Applegate put their heads together and designed a much-improved fighting knife, which unfortunately didn't become available until long after the war. In 1980, almost twenty years after Fairbairn's death, Col. Rex Applegate decided to put their improved design — known as the "Applegate-Fairbairn" — into production. The result was a fighting dagger with none of the drawbacks associated with the Fairbairn-Sykes. It has a wider, stronger blade for deeper slashing that will not snap at the tip or tang, perfect balance and a grip that provides positive blade orientation when drawing without looking.

Another excellent fighting dagger to evolve out of WWII was the Randall Model #2 "Fighting Stiletto". In essence, the #2 is an improved and strengthened version of the Fairbairn-Sykes, without its previously-mentioned design flaws. The Randall #2 continues to be one of the most popular custom fighting knives available today.

During the 1960s, new versions of the fighting dagger appeared in the guise of survival knives: like the Gerber Mark 1 and Mark 2. These were very popular with troops in Vietnam, and in turn, spawned a new generation of survival daggers featuring spear or drop point designs. Because they have narrow blades and double edges, some of these survival daggers will make good fighting knives. Even if they have saw teeth along one or both edges, these will still inflict nasty slashing wounds in a fight.

SUMMATION:
The Dagger for Civilian Self-Defense

Although the dagger-type combat knives used by American fighting men during the first half of this century left a lot to be desired, I have tried to illustrate the basic advantages they have over Bowies as a pure fighting weapon. Certainly, a decent fighting Bowie design is more valuable for self-defense than a poorly-made dagger. But in general, the dagger is easier to conceal, better for thrusting and sharpened on both edges for maximum slashing potential. For the urban civilian, the dagger is clearly the better choice for personal protection.

One of the newest Gerber survival knives, the TAC-II (right), comes with a molded sheath and a spring loaded push button release for rapid deployment.

Below is Robert Parrish's "Survivor," which includes three rows of saw teeth, a hollow handle for storage and a sharpened, modified spear point for slashing and stabbing.

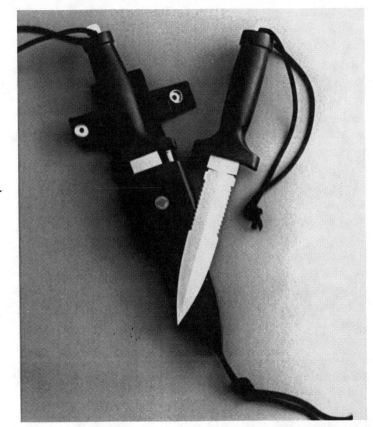

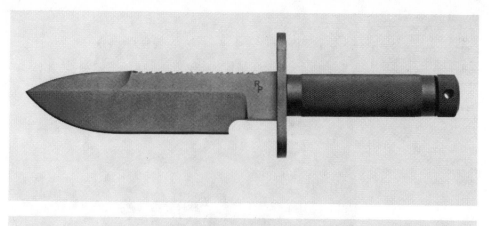

On top is the "Sunfish", virtually the same as the "Survivor" except for its shorter size and broad drop point, while the Model 36 (middle) features the same design minus the saw teeth.

Opposite page, one of the most beautiful and functional fighters around, the Browning Damascus Classic Fighter. Handle is Cocobolo, blade is composed of over 200 layers of nickel and stainless steel.

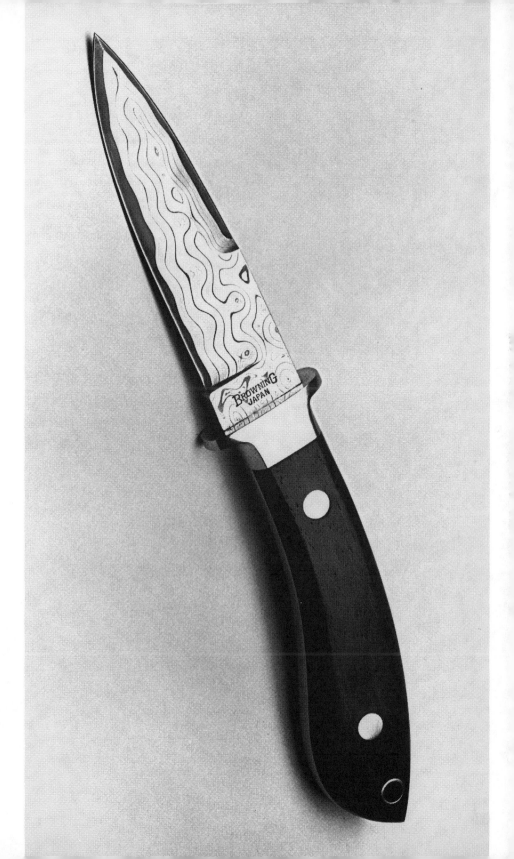

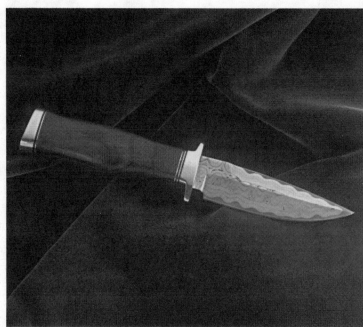

Although designed as a limited edition hunter, the author feels that this double-edged Browning with Damascus steel blade (left) makes an excellent small fighter.

Below, this unique double-edged dagger –reminiscent of an "Arkansas Toothpick" –from Phill Hartsfield is fashioned from high-speed tool steel and ground to a razor's edge on one side only!

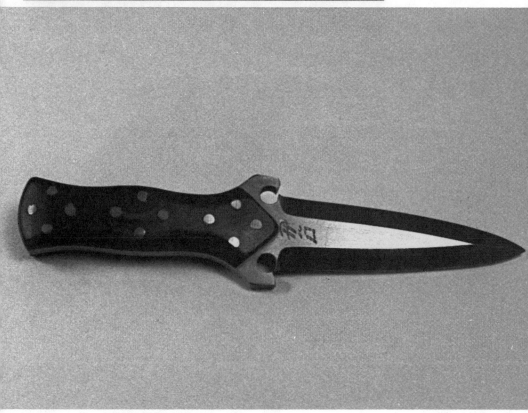

Double-edged knives from Robert Terzuola: Two versions of the "Combat Master". Top blade features a polished blade, stainless bolsters and wood grip, while bottom version sports a matte blade and micarta grip. Below them is one of Terzuola's latest fighters, the "Battle Mate" with a 7 inch blade, nickle guard and "hypergrip" cushioned handle.

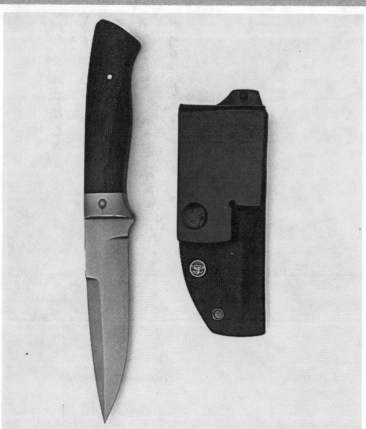

The two versions of the "Battle Guard" (above) were designed especially for the U.S. Special Forces with micarta handles and a polished steel or parkerized blade finish. One of Terzuola's short-blade fighters is the "Athena" (left), a drop point double-edged dagger with no cross guard that's easy to conceal.

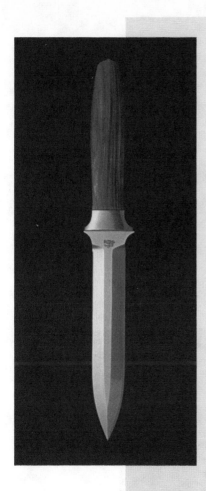

The "Madeleine"
(above) bears a close
resemblance to the
Fairbairn-Sykes with
its sleek stiletto blade
and foil-shaped handle.
All of Terzuola's
knives are excellent
buys.

Another exceptional
double-edged fighter
is the "Fer-de-lance"
(right), designed by
David Steel for Pacific
Cutlery. This knife is
made from a solid
piece of stainless steel
with pinned micarta
handle slabs, which
some find to be too
slender and slippery.

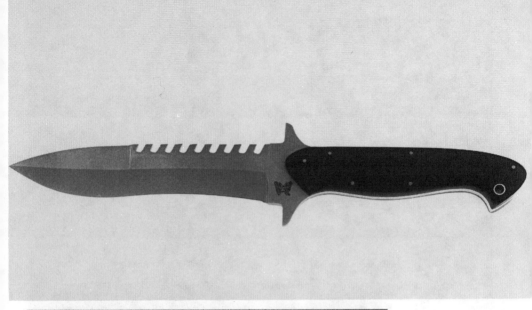

The "Timba" survival knife from Pacific Cutlery (top), is also made from a single piece of stainless with sharpened top edge, saw teeth and "Plow" handle.

The Tekna stainless survival dagger (left) is composed of a solid piece of steel with a skeletonized handle to reduce weight. Although primarily design for use underwater or near marine environments, the Tekna also provides some excellent features for combat.

Pat Crawford specializes in combat knives, particularly double-edged dagger designs like the coffin handled "Assassin" (top), sub-hilted "Battle Bowie" (2nd from top) with plow handle, followed by the "Battle Dirk" with grooved handle, and lastly, the same "Battle Dirk" with sub-hilt.

The fine lines of a Crawford blade are also visible in his boot knives (right). From top to bottom: the "Surefire", "Spider", "Point Blank" and 'Quick Draw" models.

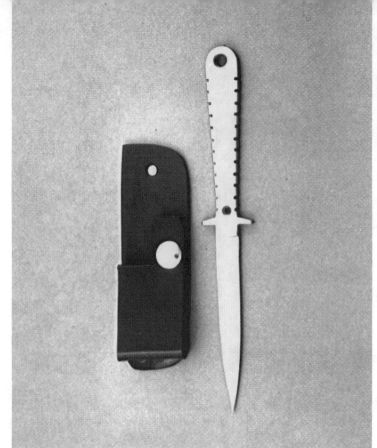

One of Crawford's smallest fighters is the "Hideout" (left), a bead blasted, hollow ground knife that sports a razor sharp edge. His "Special Fighter" (below) comes minus a crossguard, with a 7" hollow-ground blade and a black micarta handle.

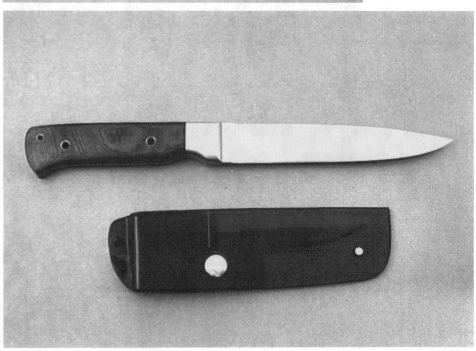

Crawford also makes "artsy" collector's pieces like these "Assassin Combat Stilettos" with staghorn, cocobolo and fancy micarta coffin handles. Although not his specialty, Crawford will also make custom survival knives, like this unique double-edge design (below) featuring saw teeth and a pistol butt grip.

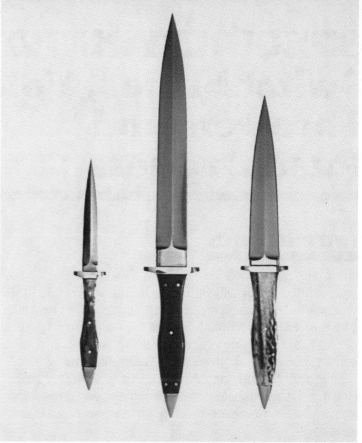

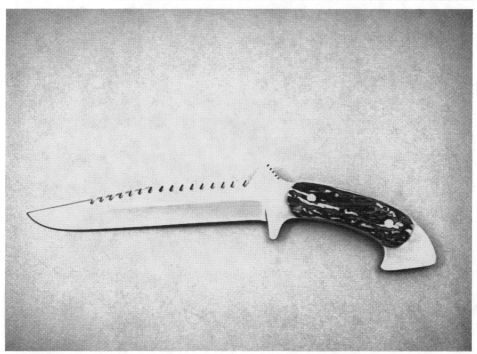

SPECIALTY KNIVES:
Switchblades, Folders, Throwers and Push Daggers

SWITCHBLADES

It's almost impossible to say anything GOOD about switchblades or gravity knives. During the 1950's, the switchblade was identified with street gangs and juvenile violence, leading to a subsequent ban on their importation from abroad. Somehow, the politicians figured that banning these cheap, ineffective weapons would reduce juvenile street crime. Instead, the ban made switchblades even more desireable to impressionable young punks who became overly fascinated with push buttons and clicking blades.

Most switchblades or gravity knives are imported from Italy, Spain and the Far East. They are made of cheap materials, are lousy for fighting, and usually wear out

If it's a choice between cheap foreign switchblades and steak knives, the author would select kitchen cutlery like these offerings from Buck. Most kitchen knives have better handles, stronger blades and sharper edges than a cheap switchblade.

quickly. Dirt or lint from in-pocket carry will jam up the springs, the cheap blades are easily snapped and hard to sharpen, and the handles are generally made for containing the blade, not for wielding it.

Sure, switchblades are potentially lethal, but if I had a choice between an Italian switchblade and a kitchen knife, I'd take the latter. If you ever have the misfortune to face a knife attacker, there are two things you should wish for: First, hope that he learned everything he knows about knives from old Sal Mineo and James Dean movies. And second, hope that he's using a switchblade instead of a REAL fighting knife. 'Nuff said.

FOLDERS

Three folding, lightweight knives from Al Mar. He titles them his "Airweights."

Although there are several companies that manufacture excellent folders and lock-back knives these days, it is not wise to rely on them for "frontline" self-defense use. Sure, they can be used to thrust or slash in a pinch, but that's not what they were designed for. The blades are usually single-edged and not long enough for hitting vital organs with a thrust. Lack of weight and a narrow blade

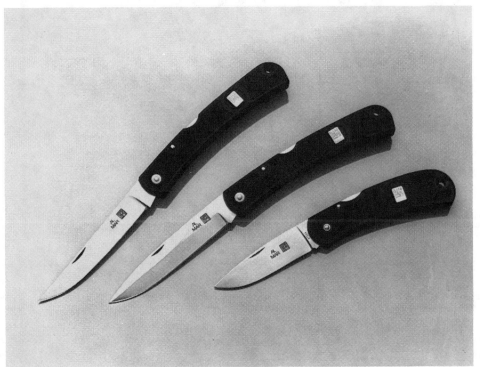

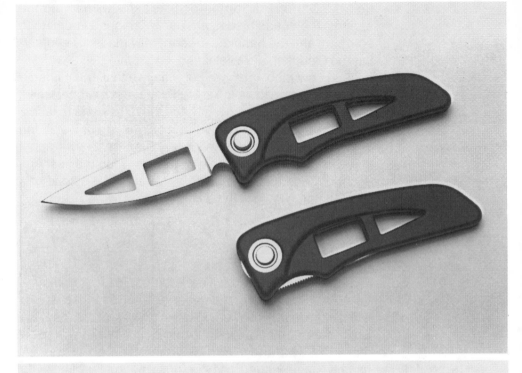

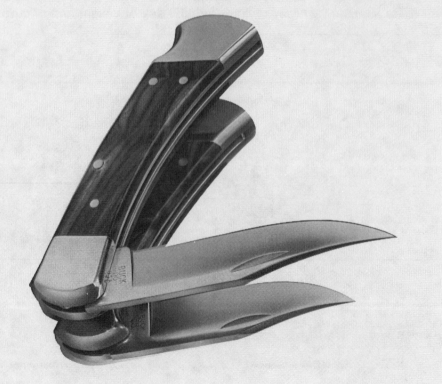

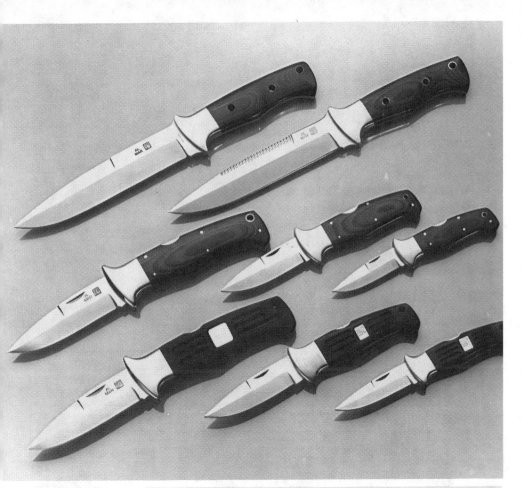

Most light utility folders like the Al Mar Airweights or the "Hidden Edge" button-lock knife from Tekna (opposite top) make excellent pocket knives but are too light and small to rely on for self-defense. Even the hardy Buck "Ranger" and "Hunter" folders (opposite bottom) feature a design more useful in the field than on the streets. Some knife makers are now offering folders with combat capabilities. Above, six knives are Al Mar folding "SERE" models with either micarta or neoprene handles. (Top two fixed-blades are SERE Model VI in combat and survival versions.) Right, Cold Steel offers it's unique new "Shinobu Tanto" lock-backs in three sizes.

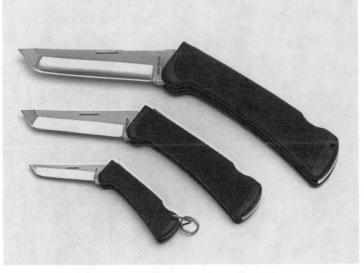

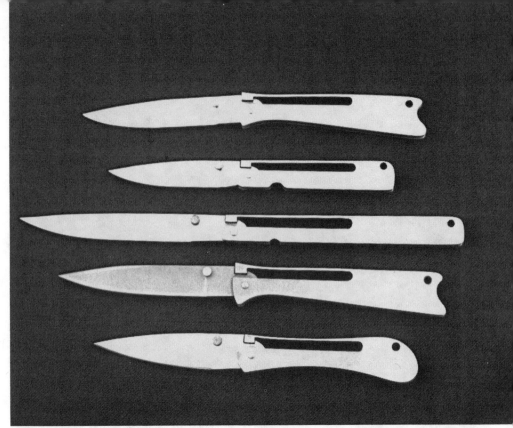

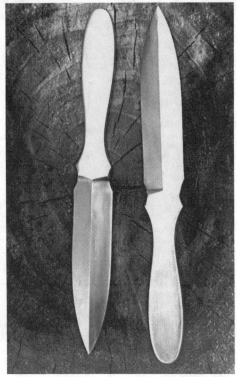

Custom maker Pat Crawford designed these solid-steel "frame-lock folders" that can be opened one-handed (opposite top). Bottom left, a professional throwing knife designed by Harry McEvoy of Tru-Balance Knives: This large, heavy knife has unsharpened edges but is balanced for flight, not fighting! Many throwing knife designs are solid stainless with no handles, like the pair from the Bowen Knife Company (bottom right). Since throwers take a lot of abuse during practice, wooden or other type grips are omitted to avoid constant breakage.

shape limit their ability to slash. Handles are made to cover the blade, not to fight with, and there is no cross-guard to keep your hand from sliding up the edge.

One of the most important aspects of knife fighting is being able to get the knife out FAST! If you carry a folder in your pocket, you may end up fumbling for it in a crisis. If you do get it out in time, you've still got to get it open. Even if you carry a lock-back folder in a belt sheath, the same holds true: unsnap the cover, withdraw the knife and try to get it opened before an attacker cuts you to ribbons or beats you to death with a tire iron.

Folders serve as good back-up weapons, especially if your front-line defense is a handgun, but it you intend to rely on a knife for your personal defense, a fixed blade fighter is really the best choice.

THROWERS

Many people have a fascination with throwing knives. So long as it's done for the fun of it, knife throwing is a fine sport. But for combat in the real world, it's an absolute absurdity that can get you killed — possible with your own knife after your target picks it up and comes after you with it!

Contrary to the fiction depicted in movies and on TV, it is almost impossible to kill a determined attacker by throwing your knife at him. To begin with, most knife fights occur at such close ranges that there's simply no room to wind up and throw. Secondly, a knife flying through the air spins end-over-end, requiring precise distancing in order to be sure that the knife will impact the target with the point first. For most people, it takes a distance of about five paces for a one-spin throw, 8 paces for two-spins, and so on. In the heat of a fight, you sure as Bejesus don't have time to pace off the right distances! If you are even slightly off, the knife may bounce off your enemy and make him very angry; you may as well have handed him your weapon for all the good throwing it will do you.

Good throwing knives are designed for FLIGHT, not FIGHTS. And if you carry a blade that throws well, it probably isn't a good thrusting or slashing knife. Throwers must be properly balanced: Handle throwers are blade-heavy, blade throwers handle-heavy. A blade thrower

would be doubly foolish for combat. First you'd have to draw it by the handle, then switch to gripping it by the blade in order to throw. Forget it.

Most of the best throwing knives are also very heavy in order to get good penetration. A general rule for the throwers is a weight of one ounce per inch of length. This makes for heavy, large knives, which are not easily concealed. Another thing to remember, few professional throwers have sharpened blades; they have stout points for sticking, but the blades themselves lack a cutting edge. You might be able to stab an attacker with a thrower, but if you use the edge, you'll have to beat him to death with it 'cause it won't cut!

If you MUST carry some sort of throwing blade, I recommend the "Atchison Thrower" or some of the heavier Chinese throwing "stars". These four-or-more tipped weapons will penetrate at almost any range (although the Chinese stars and Japanese shuriken are not usually lethal due to their short blade length). There are several fine books on stars and shuriken, and I refer you to these for further readings.

A good fighting knife is not usually a good thrower, so don't disarm yourself by throwing away your knife. Period!

These two knives from Tru-Balance are hefty enough for throwing or fighting. Top blade is the "Bowie Axe" which could easily lop off limbs. Bottom knife is the "Battle Bowie" with sharpened straight-clip point.

PUSH DAGGERS

The push dagger (often called a "push knife" or "push dirk") is probably THE most underrated self-defense blade around. Most books on knife fighting dismiss it with a few sentences, or at most, a paragraph. It is seldom considered as a serious fighting implement, even though it was used extensively during the 1800's by well-dressed gentlemen in the South who found it easily concealable and quick to bring into action.

Push daggers are particularly valuable for students of karate or kung-fu, since they can be easily incorporated into unarmed self-defense systems. Because this weapon is generally ignored in most works on knife fighting, I have included an entire chapter on push dagger use in Part II.

The push-dagger and derringer pistol were favorite weapons of frontier gamblers and Southern gentlemen.

Two of the best push daggers available today are the Urban Skinner (right) and the longer double-edged "Terminator" from Cold Steel Inc.

SELECTING A COMBAT KNIFE: How to Evaluate Your Needs

Regardless of what type of knife you decide on for personal protection, there are a few other important factors to consider. They are: What type of concealed carry position and sheath would best suit your needs? Do you want to buy a relatively inexpensive production knife of good quality, or would you rather have one custom-crafted by a master blademaker? What sort of finish is best — stainless, matte, blued or parkerized? And what about sharpening and long-term care?

Concealed Carry and the Sheath

Although most people concentrate on the type of knife they carry, where you carry it and how quickly you can get it into action is actually a MORE IMPORTANT consideration in the long run. The best fighting knife in the world isn't worth diddly if you're clubbed to death before you can get it out of your boot.

Everybody who is into knives these days seems to have an opinion about the "best" place to carry a knife. I don't have an opinion — I have a RULE! *If you can't carry the knife in your hand, it should be concealed in a place that allows you to carry it comfortably and draw it INSTANTLY.*

What is right for some knife expert may not be right for you. You have to consider factors like: your build, how you dress, having access to the blade in different positions (standing, sitting, when grabbed from behind, etc.) and your reflex speed and agility. I have a friend who can

Keeping a knife in your boot may get you a kick in the chops and a broken neck if you're caught by surprise while drawing it. The shoulder carry using a harness is very practical if you usually wear some sort of coat.

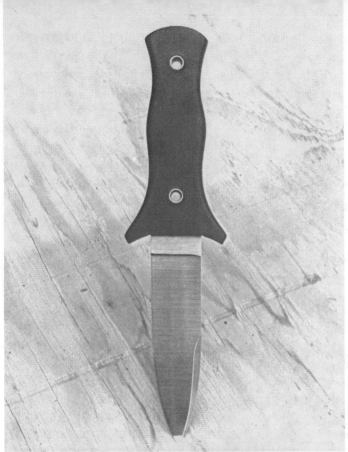

Close up of the
"Ninja" knife
illustrates its anti-snag
guard configuration.
The sheath on the
Applegate-Fairbairn
fighting knife has
eyelets for sewing it
into clothing or for
dangling it upside
down in a chest-carry
position.

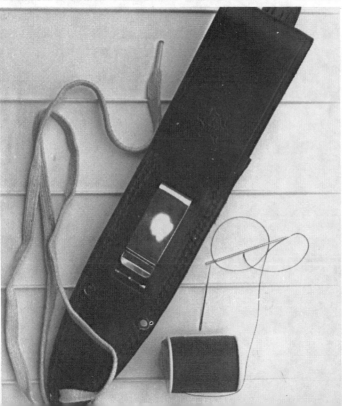

lift his front leg the instant he senses trouble and withdraw his bootknife WITHOUT bending over, and he can do it in a blink of an eye. Most people would fall over backwards if they tried to do such a thing. BUT IT WORKS FOR HIM. What's "wrong" for one might be "perfect" for another. This is an evaluation that should be made after becoming familiar with some of the following basic types of concealed carry.

For most people, the boot carry is too slow and difficult to consider. Bending over and pulling up your pant leg when under attack leaves you too vulnerable to a kick in the chops or knife in the back. Besides, who wears high-top boots everyday? Not me! Ever try to slide a boot knife inside a pair of Nikes?

There are a lot of strange opinions about the chest carry, which can be a good position for some individuals. There are two basic types of chest carry; the shoulder rig carry (with the knife off to one side) and the dangling carry (where the knife dangles upside down from a string harness around the neck). Each has its own application.

If you spend a lot of time wearing jackets or suit coats, you may find the shoulder rig carry to be best. With this method, you can leave your jacket unbuttoned most of the time without exposing your weapon to casual viewers. You definitely can't do this with a dangling chest carry unless you wear it beneath a shirt, and then you will have to fumble with your shirt buttons to get to the knife. Not very practical.

The chest carry, with the knife hanging upside down, is probably the best for UNCONCEALED carry. If you wear windbreakers or zipper type coats, the knife can be concealed but still accessed quickly by unzipping with the weak hand and drawing with the strong hand. If you suddenly sense trouble, you can inconspicuously unzip your jacket to quicken your draw.

Another possible place for a coat-wearer is in a horizontal position on the back of the belt. Several companies make swivel sheaths that can be worn in this way. If you spend a lot of time sitting, however, this could prove to be uncomfortable. It would also make it virtually impossible to draw the blade from a seated or prone position.

If you wear heavy clothing like coveralls a great deal, consider Fairbairn's thigh pocket carry. You can cut out

If you wear loose-fitting, long jackets you might consider a full-sized combat knife like this Smith & Wesson Police Bowie on a belt carry sheath. Sheath and knife can be removed quickly from the belt with a snap.

One of the problems with the belt carry is this – you can't get to it quickly if you button the coat. Below, a unique hideaway knife is the "Last Friend" from Jerry Price. This one-piece Parkerized blade is curved to fit into a special sheath that can be velcro'ed INSIDE the waistband of your pants.

The simple pocket carry: While distracting your attacker you can quickly withdraw a push dagger for a surprise counter before he can react.

If you can't easily conceal a knife and have to travel through dangerous areas, consider hiding the knife in a paper bag and carrying it inconspicuously like a parcel. When attacked, simple slash or thrust right through the paper.

In warm weather, concealing a knife—ANY knife—can be a problem. One of the best hideaway knives is the Bowen belt buckle knife (right), modeled on the opposite page by the author. By popping the tongue of the belt, the buckle can be withdrawn in a corkscrew grip, and put into immediate defensive action along with the belt itself, which can be used as a net or whip against an opposing blade.

One of the best carries is up the sleeve of loose-fitting coats or longsleeved shirts. You can easily make your own forearm sheath at home with rivets, snaps and purse leather as shown below.

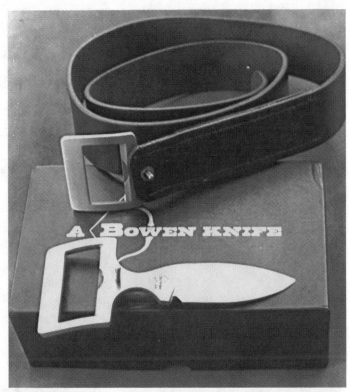

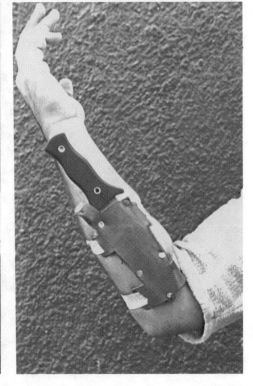

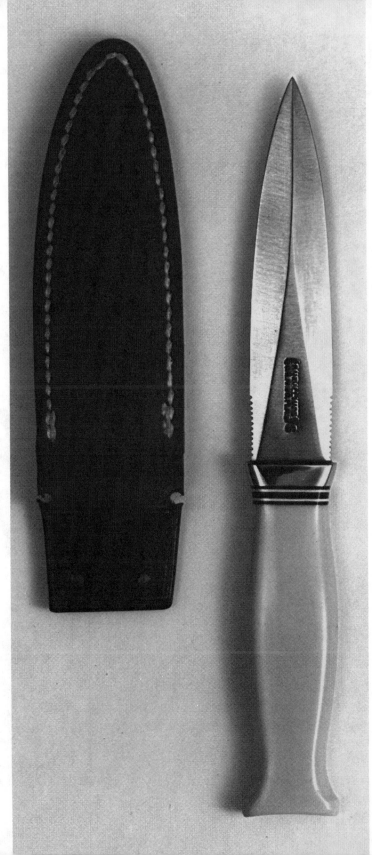

Some good designs for sleeve carry include the guardless Gerber (opposite top), designed by R.W. Loveless; below it is the Smith & Wesson boot knife. Another is this beautiful Randall #24 with a scabbard that can be modified for forearm carry (right).

The behind-the-neck carry is highly overrated for street defense because most modern clothing makes it difficult—or almost impossible—to get to quickly.

Most modern fighters feature two types of release—the snap (bottom) or the velcro quick break (top).

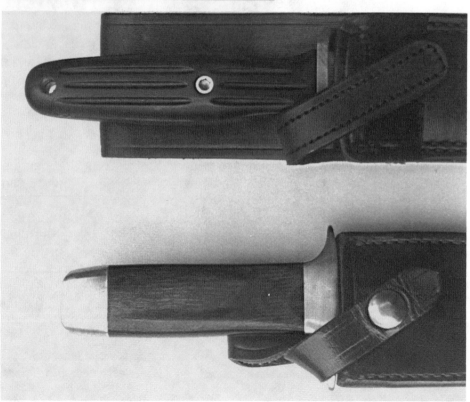

Don't let the design of the sheath determine the manner of carry—the plastic kydex sheath that comes with this fine "Combat Master" by Robert Terzuola would not be suited to several types of carry.

the bottom of your front pocket and stitch a sheath into it for a very casual, yet surprising quick draw. Try to sew the sheath in a position that allows access when seated as well as when standing. This wouldn't work well for a business suit, however, since the thin, pressed pants material would "print" the knife outline during routine movement.

There is nothing wrong with a standard, strong-side or cross-draw belt carry, providing you can conceal the entire sheathed blade, and only if you can get the concealing clothing out of the way fast enough for a quick draw. If you wear zippered or button clothes, you will have to unfasten them first to get to the blade; the same as you would have to do with the chest or shoulder carry.

If you can find coats with big pockets, you can just carry the knife in whichever pocket is easiest. If you can, sew the sheath inside the pocket, or simply put masking tape over the edges of the blade and carry it bare. So long as the edges are taped, you won't cut yourself or the cloth pocket, yet the thin tape will do nothing to impede the knife's slashing and stabbing capacity.

One of the very best carries is up the sleeve of a coat or loose shirt. Accesses from a sheath attached to the forearm is quick, inconspicuous and possible from several positions. It's also pretty comfortable for all day carry. All you have to do is wear something with long sleeves.

Another possible carry, and one I think is overrated for civilian use, is the behind-the-neck position. Unless the pommel sticks out above the collar of your shirt, AND coat, you'll look pretty funny groping around behind your head for the handle. This would be excellent for an UNCONCEALED carry, but I question its versatility for civilian use in modern American society. When you consider how tightly men's clothing fits across the shoulders these days, it's hard to see how you could successfully conceal a knife in this position and still get to it INSTANTLY.

Once you've decided which carry — or carries — are best for you, determine whether the stock sheath for the knife will work that way. DO NOT let the design of the sheath determine how you carry the weapon; if the knife is ideal, but the sheath is lacking, get another sheath or have the stock sheath modified. You can even make your own sheath if you're handy. There are also holster and knife companies that make shoulder harnesses for a variety of sheath designs, should you desire to carry the knife that way.

Another important aspect of the sheath is the release. Most of today's fighting knives offer Velcro-type "quick break" straps, or a simple snap. Other knives, designed strictly for belt carry, rely on blade-to-sheath fit for retention. If your knife has such a sheath, and you decide to use a chest or shoulder carry, you will need to add a retaining strap of some sort. An elastic thong that can be quickly thumbed off would also be a feasible substitute for a leather strap, if you prefer.

Three beautiful custom blades from Jack Crain; the "Life Support System" (left), "Scorpion" (center) and "Commando", all in stainless steel.

Custom vs. Production

While I do not mean to belittle the skills of custom knifemakers, it's quite possible to purchase an excellent production fighter for less than $150 these days. Keep in mind the designs for some of the best fighting blades around were created by custom knifemakers who spent years working on handmade prototypes, but once a particular design is "down pat," there is really nothing substantially different between a production process blade and the handmade knife. Both use the same carbon or Stainless steels, but the grinding and finishing, which takes a custom maker hours or days, can be completed with

The best fighting knives around—production or custom—were originally designed by hardworking custom knifemakers like Pat Crawford. Here we see just some of the facets of Pat's work, from planning (left) to grinding (below), to delicate filing (opposite top) and finally, the finished product.

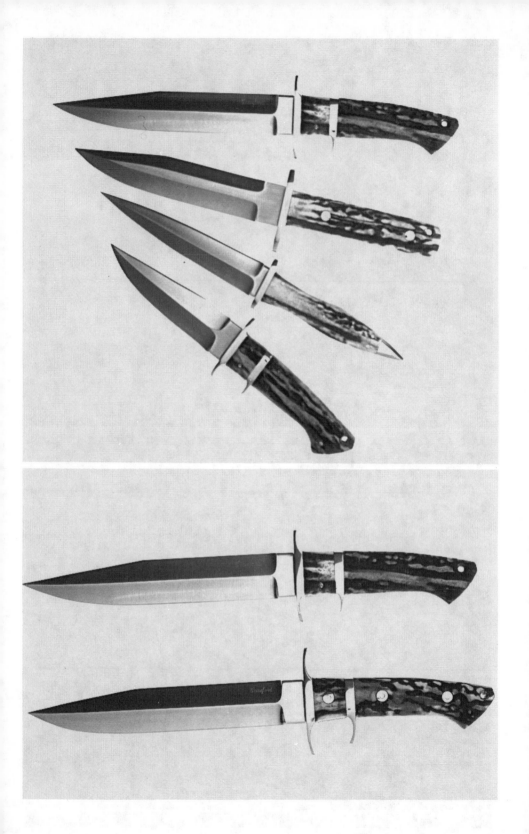

Some things you can't get on a production knife are your own modifications and specially requested materials, like these stag handles on some Crawford fighters. Something else you won't see on many production pieces: "sub-hilt"guards for extra leverage and a better grip (opposite). You also won't find the unique lines, single-side grind, pistol grip handles or cut-out crossguards of a Phill Hartsfield blade on any production fighter. Above, from top to bottom, the "Force 3" with Zebrawood grips; a variation of the "Force 3" with cocobolo grips; a "Force 1" with wrapped cord; and a "Force 1" with cocobolo grips.

machine processes in minutes. The differences in cost between the two should be obvious.

Some custom makers, like Randall, have managed to keep the cost of their fighting knives down without resorting to die stamping methods. Their famous Models #1 and #2, both hand forged and shaped, list at less than $160 apiece. Although Randall and others claim no commercial tempering process can rival hand forging, recent blades produced in Japan are, in my opinion, every bit as sharp as those on a Randall or other custom knife. What you CAN'T get from anyone else is the often imitated, but never duplicated, Randall design; *the Randall #1 is probably the best modified Bowie ever made for fighting.*

One advantage of the handmade knife is that you can choose custom design features unavailable with factory knives (special blade lengths, wood or horn handles, sharpened or lengthened false edges, modified sheaths, etc.). Most custom makers offer catalogs of various designs along with priced options — you get what you're willing to pay for! One drawback to this is the waiting time. Many of the best custom makers are backed up years with prepaid orders. My newest Randall catalog states delivery can't be guaranteed within TWO YEARS!

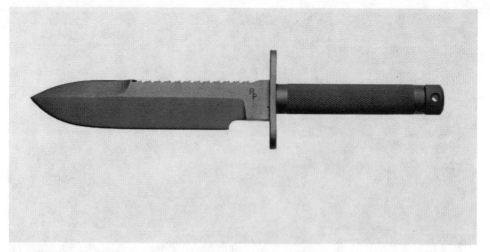

Knife Finishes

Almost all custom makers and most of the commercial producers are now offering their fighters in both Stainless and carbon steel. Some companies, like Gerber, offer blades of electrostatically-coated "black Stainless" that will neither rust nor reflect light in the dark.

For fighting purposes, the debate over which holds the better edge — Stainless or carbon steel — is unimportant. Both can be stoned plenty sharp for slashing purposes. Once your fighter is properly sharpened, you should NEVER use it for stripping wires, whittling pencils or anything other than fighting! Carry a pocket knife for general use so that your weapon will always be in peak readiness.

I personally prefer Stainless blades, because they do not rust. In my opinion, this is a must for a survival knife. Exposure to salt air and humidity can turn a carbon blade into a rust heap overnight, even though you try to keep it oiled and dry. And if you carry your knife close to your body, perspiration will do the same thing.

A Robert Parrish Survival/Combat knife, fashioned of 440c stainless steel for protection from the elements.

Storage and Sharpening

If you decide on a knife that is available only in carbon steel, consider blueing the blade to inhibit rust. This also makes the blade less conspicuous at night. If your knife does become rusty, remove it by gently sanding with VERY fine emery cloth, then oil it immediately. If you intend to

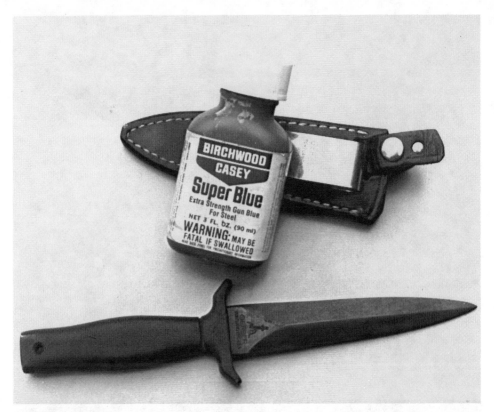

If you want to protect or darken a tool steel blade, like the one on this Gerber boot knife (above), consider using some gun bluing and a light coat of oil.

store the knife for a time, be sure to oil it generously, but DO NOT store it in its sheath. Oil will make the sheath stretch, and it will also get on your clothing when you carry it the next time. Store an oiled knife separate from its sheath.

For sharpening, first apply a dab of honing oil or light lubricant to the edges. As a sharpening tool, I recommend using a ceramic stick (It's easier to run a stick along each edge than it is to run the edges across a flat stone at the proper angle). DO NOT apply pressure when running the sharpener across the edges. Try to use clean, even strokes from the crossguard toward the tip in a file-like motion. After about four strokes on each edge, turn the blade over and repeat. Wash the ceramic stick with soap after each sharpening and clean the sharpened blade with oil. If your knife is Stainless, simply wipe clean. Try to keep oil off of the handle; it can severely damage many of the modern rubber and plastic handles, and it makes wood extremely slippery.

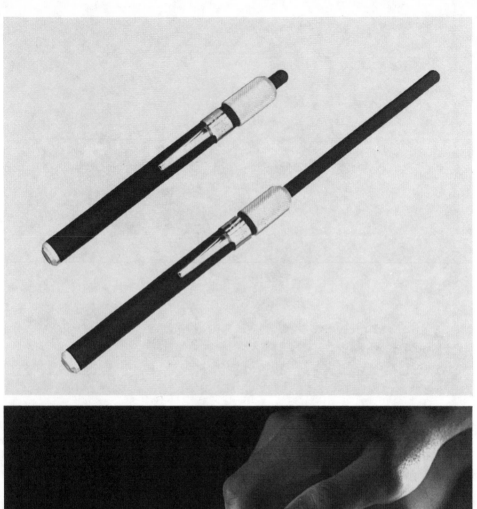

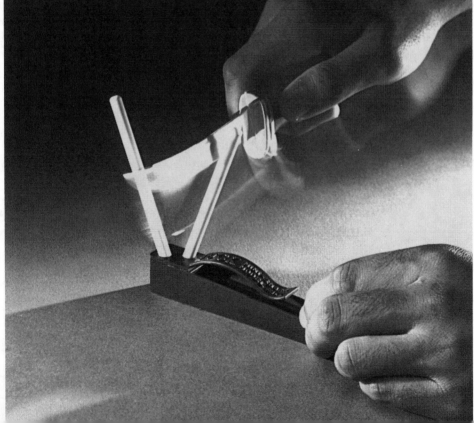

Sharpening a fighter shouldn't be something you'll have to do very often unless you misuse the knife as a utility tool. For occasional touch-up, the author prefers a ceramic stick like the "Edgemaster" from Buck (opposite bottom). A portable version of the ceramic stick is also available from Buck; the "Mini-Sharp", which will break down to fit in a pocket (opposite top). This Buck "Jiffy Sharp" (right) will also fill the bill as a touch up sharpener for most fighting knives. But for those of you who are really "into" a razor sharp edge, the author recommends this three stone "Triple Sharp" system from Buck (below).

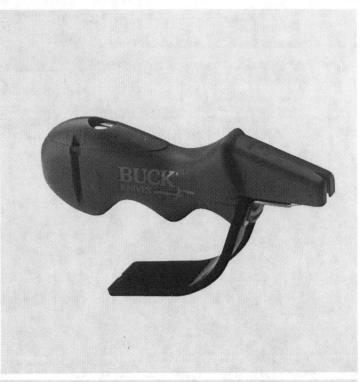

PART TWO
The Fighting Knife in Self-Defense

During the 20th Century, two major approaches to knife fighting have been dominant in America. The first is the "Shanghai School" of Fairbairn, Sykes and Applegate. These methods were taught to thousands of fighting men during and after WWII. The second was the "classical" or "formal school" advocated by A.J.D. Biddle and his student John Styres of the U.S. Marine Corps. To understand how radically different these two schools are, we will examine each of them separately.

The Shanghai SCHOOL: Fairbairn, Sykes and Applegate of the OSS

William Ewart Fairbairn spent the major portion of his life in Asia, beginning with a stint in the Royal Marine Light Infantry stationed in Korea at the turn of the century. In 1907, he left the Marines and became a constable with the Shanghai Municipal Police (SMP), which served as the law enforcement authority in the International District of China's largest city.

The Shanghai of that era was a rough-and-tumble port city. And its huge criminal element was well-versed in many refined systems of hand-to-hand and knife combat. Robberies, political kidnappings and riots were common.

Fairbairn was placed in charge of combat training for the SMP in 1910, and during the next 15 years, he insisted on personally participating in over 600 armed encounters answered by the SMP. This often placed him "on the spot" during shootouts, knife fights and all-out brawls.

At the same time, Fairbairn was an earnest student of both Chinese boxing *(pakua)* and Japanese jujitsu. He studied pakua under Tsai Ching-tunk, one-time instructor to the bodyguards of the Dowager Empress, and also received his 2nd degree black belt from the Kodokan Jujutsu University. This latter degree was bestowed by the great master Jigoro Kano, himself.

In 1925, Fairbairn published *Defendu,* his synthesis of boxing, jujutsu and other techniques derived from his first-hand combat experiences. He considered his system to be oriented towards the average Westerner. It eliminated much that was ornamental or acrobatic from the Oriental methods he had learned, while updating the techniques to deal with gun, knife and other types of armed attack.

Initially written for police, Fairbairn's work became very popular among British and American troops stationed in China before WWII. Although retired from the SMP by 1940, Fairbairn and his associate Eric Anthony Sykes (former director of the SMP's Sniper Team) were called up by the British at the outset of the war to develop a series of training facilities for the newly-created commandoes. Within a year, Fairbairn and Sykes had organized several successful schools that taught method of "unconventional" warfare to Allied commandoes, spies and saboteurs. All facets of close combat were included; Use of the handgun, knife, improvised weaponry and unarmed fighting were all part of the regimen.

In 1943, the U.S. created its very first intelligence agency, the Office of Strategic Services (OSS). Today, we know it as the CIA. The first OSS training school for spies and assassins was set up in early 1942 under the direction of Lt. Rex Applegate of the U.S. Army, a specialist in

Kill or Get Killed is currently in its 18th printing and is probably the most concise single volume on close combat ever published. Knife is an early custom version of the Applegate-Fairbairn from Yancey Knives.

Unlike Fairbairn, Applegate did not favor the use of restraints, joint locks or come-along techniques for defense against a knife.

military counterintelligence. Later that year, Fairbairn was "loaned" by the British to the OSS, where he worked closely with Applegate in standardizing and refining close-combat techniques and training procedures. In the meantime, Sykes remained in Britain to continue direction of the commando schools.

In 1943, Applegate was given a new assignment: Develop a close-combat training facility for Military Intelligence at Camp Ritchie, Maryland. Leaving Fairbairn to run the OSS schools, Applegate was given a free hand in putting together what many experts now consider to have been the most elaborate close-combat training facility ever conceived. Applegate chose only battle-hardened veterans as instructors at MITC; *men who knew what did and what did not work in the heat of combat.*

Techniques and equipment were constantly modified and improved as reports from the field dictated, and in late-1943, Applegate published one of the great classics of close combat, *Kill Or Get Killed.* Now in its 18th printing, and available in foreign languages, the book is still considered by many to be the best textbook ever written on practical close combat.

It is actually Applegate who provides us with the basic approach to knife fighting characteristic of the Shanghai School. Although much of what Applegate set forth in *Kill Or Get Killed* was vintage Fairbairn, there are some areas of disagreement. In defending against the knife, Fairbairn — the former policeman — favored the use of the submission holds he had extracted from jujutsu. Applegate favored striking techniques instead, pointing out, "The jujutsu user has to be really expert if he is to overcome a determined assault by an individual skilled in the use of blows of the hands and feet."

Types of Attack

To understand both knife attack and defense, Applegate separated basic attack typologies into three categories:

The Skilled Attack: When faced by a skilled attacker using the "saber" or fencer's grip, both thrusts and slashes in either direction are possible. Such an attacker may begin the assault from a bent-knee crouch, knife held back close to the chest, with the other arm extended forward to grab, parry or distract.

This stance makes grabs or cuts at the knife wrist by a defender extremely dangerous. It will also frustrate attempts to use improvised defenses — chairs, coats, etc. — to get at the knife without coming into close range of the blade. The skilled attacker can also launch a very powerful thrust from this position, stepping into the strike with momentum and body weight. According to Applegate, *this is the most dangerous type of knife attack to defend against, and therefore, the BEST TO USE for offense.*

The Unskilled Attacker: This attacker may use the "icepick" or "hammer" grip, both of which are more instinctive than the fencer's grip. Applegate warns, however, that grip alone is no indication of expertise; the icepick is a favorite grip of many Oriental experts, while the hammer grip is also very dangerous when used with a long-bladed weapon.

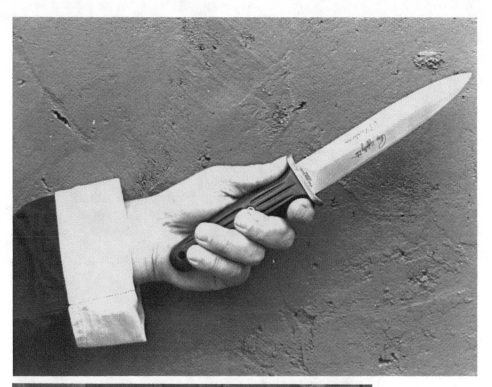

The basic "saber" grip, which Applegate considered the technique of a skilled attacker (top). The attack stance of a skilled attacker—knife hand is kept well back for stepping into a sudden thrust or slash, knees are bent and body crouched, empty hand extended to grab or parry (left). The "hammer grip" is a very instinctive grip that Applegate considered to be more common with an unskilled attacker (opposite top). This "ice pick" grip is most conducive to downward thrusts or arcing slashes and may be used by either the unskilled or "slashing" type of attacker (opposite bottom).

The "icepick" grip is most conducive to downward or overhand thrusts, while the "hammer" grip is limited to upward thrusts. Although you can slash with either grip, doing so requires wider swings because the blade is held at a 90 degree angle to the forearm. A certain amount of reach is also lost with these two grips when compared to the fencing or "saber" grip.

Applegate also felt arcing thrusts, characteristic of the icepick and hammer grips, are easier to block as opposed to the straight thrust of the saber grip, which is difficult to intercept once it is initiated.

The Slasher: this is a common form of attack in many Asian martial arts, and it is often implemented by a skilled fighter. The knife is usually held in a modified icepick grip, concealed along the forearm for sudden, surprise attacks. Horizontal slashes can be made both forehand and backhand, and they can be combined with powerful thrusts. While Applegate acknowledged that this attack can be very dangerous, he considered it inferior to that of the skilled attacker using a saber grip (due to the previously mentioned limitations of the ice pick grip).

The slashing attack usually begins with the knife held behind the forearm for concealment (1). In this sequence, female defender surprises would-be rapist with an upward slash to the jaw (2), rears back (3) and continues with an overhead downward thrust into the side of the throat (4).

Vital Targets

The Throat: This, according to Applegate and Fairbairn, is the most vital and accessible target for a knife attack. A slash or thrust below the Adam's Apple can sever the Jugular vein or major arteries, resulting in death. This is one area an opponent will defend first, however, so it may be difficult to reach.

The Abdomen: While a thrust to the heart is fatal, it is difficult to hit the heart because of the obstruction posed by the ribs. A thrust in the abdomen will produce shock, however, which should provide time to pump the knife or withdraw it for an immediate strike to the throat or kidneys.

The Kidneys: Thrusts to the kidney area, particularly from the rear as an assassination technique or for silent killing, will produce the same sort of instantaneous shock as a thrust to the abdomen. However, the kidneys must usually be attacked from behind because an assailant's elbows are usually defending it from the front.

The Limbs: These are the most easily slashed areas of the body. Slashes to the hand, wrist, forearm or biceps

NO.	NAME OF ARTERY	SIZE	DEPTH BELOW SURFACE IN INCHES	LOSS OF CONSCIOUSNESS IN SECONDS	DEATH
1	Brachial	Medium	½	14	1½ Min.
2	Radial	Small	¼	30	2 Min.
3	Carotid	Large	1½	5	12 Sec.
4	Subclavian	Large	2½	2	3½ Sec.
5	(Heart)		3½	Instantaneous	3 Sec.
6	(Stomach)		5	Depending on depth of cut	

The most lethal targets for knife defense according to Fairbairn, extracted from his book, *Get Tough*.

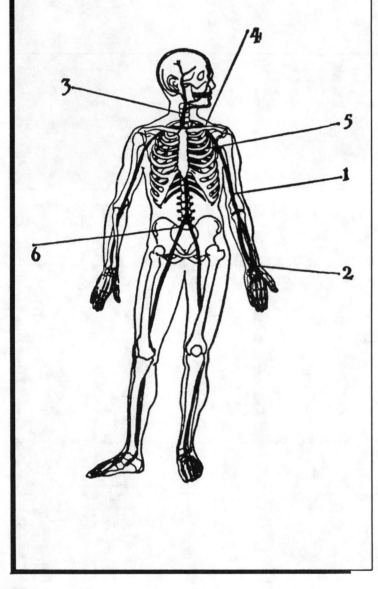

Although not lethal or always disabling, a simple slash to an attacker's limb will usually end the attack or create an opening for your escape.

will often incapacitate or cripple the limb, and they can result in death due to blood loss. A deep slash to the thigh may sever nerves and muscle needed for standing, bringing an enemy to the ground. Cutting major arteries inside the legs may result in a quick death due to bleeding.

Defense Against The Knife

Once the trainee understands the basics of knife attack, he is prepared to begin working on defenses. The first thing is to realize there is no defense against a complete surprise attack, other than not being caught by surprise to begin with! To prevent such attacks, Applegate suggested that a defender: keep his back to walls or solid objects, keep weapons and hands inconspicuously at the ready, distance himself from strangers on the street who attempt to come within blade range and wear heavy clothing resistant to slashing attacks or thrusts from short-bladed knives.

When surprised, most defenders will instinctively try to ward off an attack by throwing up his arms. This will result in some cuts, but THIS CANNOT REALISTICALLY BE AVOIDED! It is better to sustain cuts on the arms than in other, more vital areas.

The VERY BEST DEFENSE AGAINST A KNIFE AT-TACK, according to Applegate and Fairbairn, IS A GUN OR CLUB. With a gun, the attacker can be incapacitated from a distance with minimum risk to a defender. A club provides a defender more reach than the knife attacker, and it can be used to knock away the knife, break the attacker's arms or block his thrusting or slashing attacks.

If a defender is also armed with a blade, or is bare-handed, he must immediately "size up" his attacker (if time permits) and quickly resort to one of the following basic defenses:

1) Throw dirt, pocket change, a coat or even furniture into his face. If you're very close, spit in his eye — reflex will make him recoil for an instant. As soon as you make your move, either flee or reach for the nearest improvised weapon you can find. If there is nothing available, resort to a vicious kicking attack at the knife wielder's legs and shins, simultaneously leaning your upper body back and away from his knife. Once his initial assault is halted, immediately move in to deliver disabling blows to the eyes, throat or testicles.

2) Use a chair or similar object to ward the attacker off; jab the legs into his face and try to knock the blade from his grip. Drive him back into a wall, over some stairs or into furniture that will unbalance, and hopefully, trip him up.

3) Deliver an intercepting kick to his kneecap the moment he moves toward you. If your kick lands, he will likely go down, and you will be able to stomp his knife hand or kick him in the head without exposing yourself to much retaliation. Kicking, in conjunction with improvised weaponry, is also the best defense against multiple attackers. Applegate suggests that a defender back him-self into a corner so he can keep the attackers in front of him, kicking at them repeatedly as they try to move in.

4) The parry defense is useful against upward and downward thrusts, since these parries divert the attacker's arm across his body and away from the defender. Apple-gate advocates the use of parries instead of blocks. A

To prevent surprise from behind, Applegate suggested keeping your back to walls or defending from a corner (1). As attackers move in, kick to their legs to break the knee (2) while supporting yourself on the wall. By ducking and side stepping the second attacker's club, defender can now make a run for it (3).

If you've got a coat in your hand, don't try to wrap in around your arm—there won't be time and it won't stop a cut. Instead, use it to blind your attacker by throwing it into his face while you deliver a disabling counterattack.

Opposite, the parry defense is very useful against an upward thrust, since it diverts the direction of the blade away from the center of the defender's body.

Example of a parry used against an overhand icepick thrust: Defender parries thrust to the outside and downward (1-2), then unbalances the attacker with a jerk, while simultaneously smashing his liver (3).

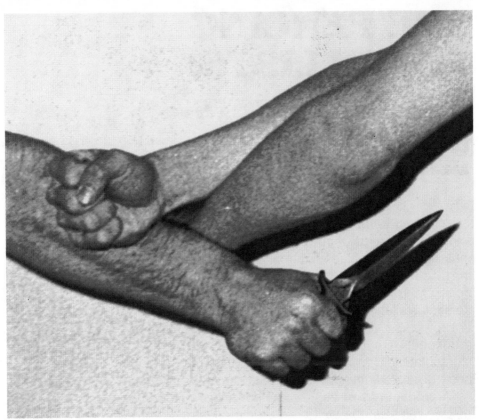

When forced to block an overhand or underhand thrust, Applegate recommended the "X-block".

parry uses the entire length of the arm for defense, does not rely solely on strength and cannot be "collapsed" like most blocks.

As soon as the parry deflects the knife, immediate counterstrikes must be launched against the assailant to put him out of action.

5) A static, blocking defense is not as reliable as a parry, but it is often required when attacked by surprise. Blocks against the knife require timing and precision, if misplaced, they may prove fatal. Trying to catch the knife wielder's wrist, or block his swing by meeting it with your forearm, requires ample light to see by and a very strong block that won't give way under the force of a thrust or slash. The only times stiff-armed blocks or wrist grabs should be used are in situations where the attacker has cocked for his delivery but not yet begun his forward surge. If forced to block a sudden overhand or underhand thrust, Applegate recommended the X-block, since it is less likely to collapse.

THE FENCING FORMALISTS: Biddle/Styers Methods

Although fencing with the knife had been taught at some of the *salles d' armes* during the 1800s, this "formal" approach to blade fighting reached its zenith under the guidance of A. J. Drexel Biddle before WWII. His 1937 book, *Do Or Die,* was one of the few guides on close combat available in America at that time, and was quickly accepted as a sort of "bible" for training by the military. In retrospect, it becomes clear that Biddle's attempt to extrapolate foil fencing technique into the realm of blood-and-guts knife fighting was a mistake.

A product of two very prominent and wealthy Philadelphia families, the well-bred Biddle spent most of his early life traveling around the world, studying sword and bayonet fencing from the great masters of Europe. In 1935 he was invited to Quantico, Virginia, to train Marine Corps officers — gentlemen all — in the arts of sword, bayonet and knife fighting.

Although known in the annals of close combat as "Lt. Col. A.J. Drexel Biddle," the title was more honorary than real, since his commission was in the Reserves and not the regular Corps. Biddle seemingly floated into and out of the Marine Corps Reserves at will, leaving many with the impression that his techniques were based on actual combat experiences. Even the fledgling FBI was impressed enough with Biddle's breeding and connections to make him the Individual Combat instructor for the Department of Justice.

There is just no kind way to say it — THE BIDDLE APPROACH TO KNIFE FIGHTING WILL GET YOU KILLED! The reality of close combat is altogether different

The influence of Biddle's teachings on the U.S. Marine Corps is clearly evidenced in their adoption of his favorite knife design, the Bowie (in the form of the Kabar), for use in the Pacific during WWII.

Left, a facsimile of the Biddle "on guard" position: Defender faces sideways, empty hand back, lead leg forward and knife hand turned with the palm upward. This works exceptionally well in sport fencing but has several drawbacks for the street. One problem with it is that it exposes the lead leg to a quick slash, kick or blow with a bludgeon, just as it did centuries ago when swords were the norm.

Below, *Passatta Sotto:* This works well with foils but not with knives. As the attacker lunges, defender merely drops low and impails him with a short thrust to the chest. To begin with, you won't get much penetration with a knife this way, and your head, neck and arm are extremely vulnerable to a downward slash if you misjudge the range.

from the gentlemanly fencing Biddle engaged in. A former Marine, who studied under Biddle, put it this way:

"The good Colonel, master swordsman, devised a fencing system FOR SWORDS. You assume the classic *En Garde* position, STICK OUT YOUR ARM AND then theoretically smite your foe with the equally classic *Hand Cut,* then skewer your opponent with the matchless *In-Quartata* and *Passata Sotto.*

"After which, in the REAL WORLD, you pick your guts up off the deck, stuff them back inside, and die like a gentleman. You were disembowelled while going into *En Garde.*"

When Biddle was called to active duty at the beginning of WWII, he tried to teach his system to Marine recruits at Parris Island and Camp Lejeune. Since "boot" Marines weren't as polite as the officers that Biddle was used to, they weren't reluctant to embarass him during training.

Sometimes they'd just skip the "En Garde" position and stick him with the knife during demonstrations. Eventually, this became so embarassing that Biddle was removed from close-combat training. More practical methods — like those devised by Fairbairn, Sykes and Applegate — replaced the Biddle system of knife fencing for the rest of the war.

The Styers Method

But the Biddle method lives on. One student of this school was former Marine John Styers, who wrote another classic on close combat, *Cold Steel,* in the early 1950s. Although the sections of Styers' book dealing with unarmed combat and stick fighting make some good points, the knife fighting techniques are classic Biddle.

Both Biddle and Styers considered the Bowie to be the ideal fighting knife. Biddle even included a rather embarassing chapter in *Do Or Die* that purported to outline the "fencing techniques" taught by Jim Bowie himself. That there is no historical record of these techniques did not seem to bother Biddle at the time. Whether he simply concocted them from imagination to prove a point or accepted them from some unreliable source will never be known, but I'd be willing to bet that Bowie would have died in his first knife fight if he'd relied on the techniques that Biddle ascribed to him.

Styers uses the same basic "on guard" stance recommended by Biddle: knife hand forward with the upper body full-facing the opponent in a duelling posture. Only the saber grip is used. To thrust, Styers relies on the pivot and torso twist used in foil fencing, weak arm thrown back as the strong arm extends forward with the blade. For defense, Styers relies solely on evasion or the defender's own blade for defense; only once is the use of a grab with the rear hand illustrated. *In every one of Styers' illustrations, there is but one attacker and always at least three feet of space between combatants.*

Styers' devotion to fencing technique is further illustrated by his attitude towards grip and stance:

"If he holds the blade...in any position other than that of a SABRE, he will definitely LIMIT the effectiveness of his RANGE. This is the predominant stance of most knife fighters throughout the world in spite of the fact that it is contrary to the 400-year-old fencing principle of keeping the RIGHT FOOT FORWARD."

Unfortunately, the romantic fencer's approach to knife fighting lives on today among many well-known blade experts who still think street combat resembles a gentlemanly, face-to-face duel. We still read about blocking knife blades with crossguards, executing "in quartata" moves after a feint and the "superiority" of the sabre grip over all others. This stuff would make a street punk from New York City double up with laughter. It simply has no bearing on reality.

The fencer's guard was devised from sport application; it was intended for hitting opponents standing in profile who NEVER changed lead sides. The fencer's linear "crab step" requires open, flat terrain and is absolutely useless against an enemy who sidesteps. And trying to parry with a knife blade IS SIMPLY INSANE! With a foil or epee, the long blade allows some room for error in parring, but with a knife blade, you will likely lose fingers and the use of your hand. NOWHERE, in either Biddle or Styers work, do we see a knife attack launched from behind or from close, grappling range. The reason for this is clear; fencing techniques will not work in MOST knife attack situations.

Both Styers and Biddle before him considered the Bowie design to be the ultimate in fighting knives. This Bowie is a Police Presentation model from S & W, no longer available. The basic ready stance of Styers is little different from that of Biddle—rear leg is turned out more, knife is held back with edge facing down, rear arm extended a bit farther forward so the body can be whipped backward as knife hand thrusts forward.

"In Quartata" is just one of the classical fencing techniques advocated by Styers. First, antagonists square off in duelling fashion (1). As fighter on left thrusts to the throat, his opponent leans to the outside and begins to shift his body around (2) in order to sidestep while simultaneously delivering a thrust to the throat (3). You've really got to try this to realize how intricate and complicated such a move would be against a short, quick blade. It might work with a sword but not in a knife fight!

3

THE MODERNIST APPROACH: Best of All Worlds

As we have seen, both the Shanghai and Formal methods were not indigenous to America. The first derived its roots from China, the second from European fencing. Americans have always been pragmatic borrowers and modifiers who take what is useful while discarding the ornamental. This is exactly what is required for a Modernist approach to knife fighting.

It is clear, from previous examination, that the Formalists have little to offer the civilian seeking practical knife fighting skills. But this does not mean the Shanghai methods are ideal, nor that they are beyond improvement. The Formalists were gentlemen knife fighters, while the Shanghai methods were intended for spies and assassins. The needs of today's civilian are in a grey area, somewhat between the two. You cannot afford to fight a sociopathic criminal like a gentleman. Likewise, you cannot dispatch him before he threatens you by stabbing him in the kidneys as if he were an enemy soldier.

The Modernist also incorporates other blade fighting methods — *iai-jutsu, kenjutsu, arnis, hwrangdo, ninjutsu* (Oriental martial art styles) and others into his repertoire if he finds that they have something to offer. Realizing that true self-defense has no "nationality," and no single "system" is perfect, the Modernist tries to fashion an approach that constitutes the best of all worlds.

The Role Of Empty-Hand Training

One of the greatest shortcomings of the Formal School is its emphasis on approaching knife fighting AS IF it were

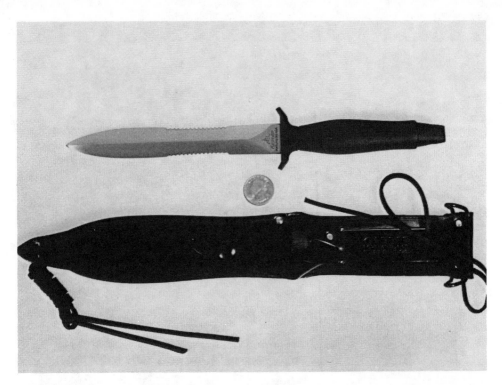

Although designed as a survival knife, the Gerber Mark II proved to be among the most popular knives carried by troops during the Vietnam War.

a separate skill from unarmed combat. Relying ONLY on the knife in a close-combat situation limits your chances for survival. The knife should be viewed as an EXTENSION of unarmed skills, not a system SEPARATE from them!

Self-defense is a composite skill. The individual who depends ONLY on weapons will be helpless if his knife or gun is taken away, dropped in a scuffle or impossible to draw in time. Likewise, the person who relies ONLY on unarmed techniques cannot realistically hope to survive armed attacks and those involving multiple assailants.

Most traditional karate and kung-fu systems take this complete approach to self-defense, offering weapons training to students who have learned the basics of hand-to-hand combat. But the Modernist realizes that in today's world, it is not practical to train with outmoded weapons like the sai, tonfa, broadsword or three-sectioned staff. The front-line weapons in 20th Century America are the handgun, knife and bludgeon. After learning unarmed techniques, these are the types of weapons the Modernist learns to use and defend against.

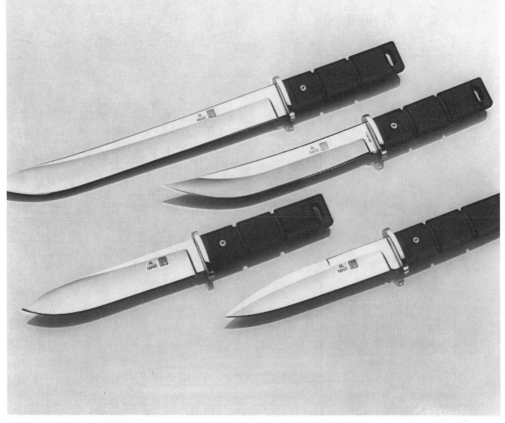

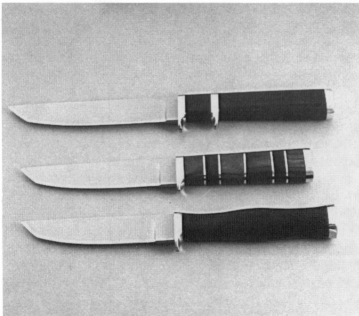

The "Modernist Approach" recognizes the value of Western AND Eastern knife fighting arts as well as knife designs, like these "Tanken" models from Al Mar (above). Several American custom makers now offer Tanto designs, like these from Pat Crawford (left). From the Phillipines arts like kali and arnis, along with knife designs like these balisongs from Pacific Cutlery (opposite), may prove invaluable to the Modernist knife fighter.

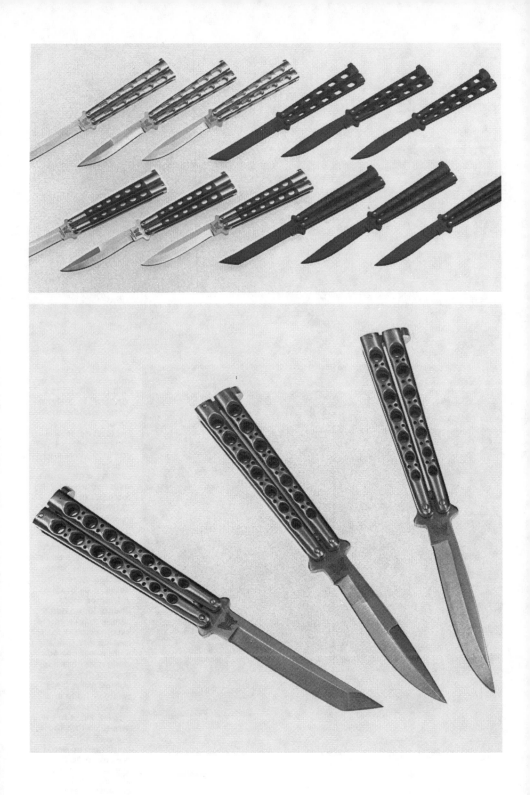

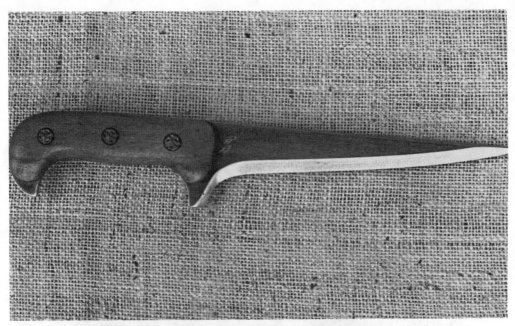

A unique, Asian-influenced design by Phill Hartsfield: His "Choora" is designed for penetrating mail armor.

For total defense, armed as well as unarmed skills are required. Just carrying a gun won't insure your safety if you can't draw it BEFORE your life is threatened.

One of the most effective Modernist Approaches is that of COMBATO, a street-oriented system founded by Bradley J. Steiner. Here, Steiner illustrates a simple knife fighting kata, using the icepick grip. Initially, knife is concealed while other hand is used to distract (1); immediately, body twists as knife arcs forward for an upward slash to the face (2). From there, the weapon continues upward (3), only to come down with a powerful thrust into the throat or collarbone area (4).

Modernist Blade Techniques

Once you've mastered the basics of unarmed combat, you can begin to incorporate blade techniques into your self-defense training. It is my personal opinion that the Shanghai School provides the most realistic FOUNDATION for knife training. Actual knife fights are more closely related to the "up close and dirty" techniques of Fairbairn, Sykes and Applegate than to the Formalists or most Asian arts that emphasize face-to-face, one-on-one duelling as a training regimen.

Because the Shanghai methods are not incorporated into a closed "system" as such, there is room for the Modernist to experiment and modify without "invalidating" the underlying principles on which the methods are based. You can't do this with rigid, systematic approaches. The Formalist approach, for example, simply won't work if you decide that keeping your knife in the rear hand is best. The entire system of fencing is predicated on having the knife hand forward. If you violate this requirement, you can't fence with a knife. Period.

The Shanghai methods are neither dogmatic nor highly systematized. The civilian knife fighter has to realize they were initially designed for military application, and he must modify them to fit his own needs. Most of the basic techniques, however, are very effective "as is;" the block, parry and chair defenses, the grips, target areas and footwork of the Shanghai school have not been substantially improved upon in the last 43 years. If you can successfully integrate those techniques with your unarmed karate or kung-fu training, you are indeed a practitioner of the Modernist School of knife fighting.

Here, Steiner illustrates a defensive technique designed by Fairbairn and incorporated into Combato. Using a chair against an aggressive attacker will not only hold him at bay (1), but may be used to deliver disabling strikes, like this eye poke with the chair leg (2).

113

Because criminals who attack with a knife will likely choose victims who are physically weaker, Combato does not use restraint techniques like this attempted "figure four armlock" (1), which is difficult to apply against a stronger assailant (2), possibly resulting in death or serious injury to the defender (3).

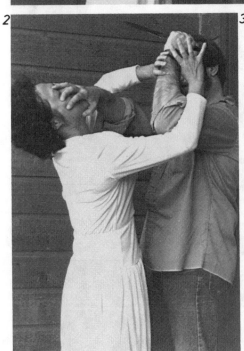

In a Modernist system like Combato, tactics like surprise, deception and distraction are stressed. Here, a female victim attempts to placate her attacker while keeping the knife concealed behind here rear leg (1); delivering a side kick to the knee as her attacker comes in range (2), the defender cocks her left hand for a strike to his throat (3) and then finishes him off with a thrust to the chest (4). This sequence illustrates the importance of unarmed techniques as adjuncts to the knife as a defensive weapon.

115

1

The stick is also considered an effective modern weapon in Combato. It has several advantages over the knife for defense. As attacker thrusts (1), defender parries his entire arm with the stick (2), then uses the stick's pointed end to incapacitate the attacker with a smash to the throat (3).

2

3

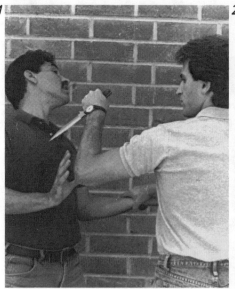

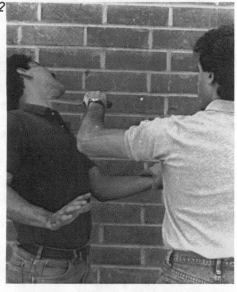

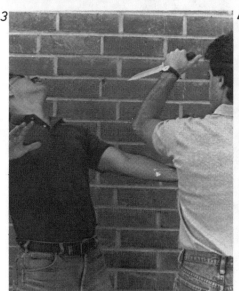

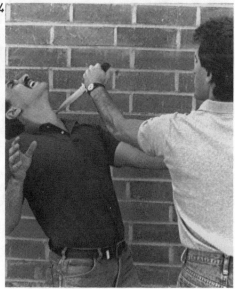

One thing that Eastern systems stress more than those of the West is the slash defense, using the icepick grip. This is a highly versatile move. The knife comes up from either the draw or a concealed position (1), then arcs toward the throat like a hook punch (2). As knife blade cuts and continues by (3), the swing is reversed for either a backhand slash or stab into the throat (4).

The Modernist School also recognizes the importance of improvised weapons, since most knife attacks will occur without warning, possibly from behind (1); even a piece of scrap lumber makes a good defense against a knife attack if you can think and act quickly (2).

If you've studied primarily Asian self-defense systems, you should devise defenses against Western types of knife attacks, like this straight thrust to the abdomen. Defender sidesteps and parries with the forearm (1), then delivers an immediate backhand blow to the head (2), followed by a palm smash to the jaw (3).

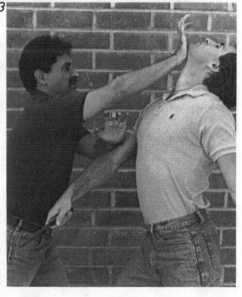

Exercises for the knife fighter should strengthen the wrists (top) and the forearms (bottom) with various forms of resistance training.

For training with live partners, I recommend this rubber Applegate-Fairbairn from All Mar (opposite page). It has a wide edge that can be chalked for realistic practice.

The Fighting Push Daggers

Push daggers and derringer pistols were the favorite concealed weapons carried by gamblers, gentlemen and rogues of the 19th Century American Frontier. As civilization crept westward after the Civil War, it became increasingly unacceptable for gentlemen to saunter about with large Colt revolvers and Bowie knives on their belts. A need arose for smaller guns and knives that could be hidden in a pocket or slipped up a coat sleeve.

The push dagger design is unique from other knives in that its handle is mounted perpendicular to the blade, instead of in line with it. This T-shape allows the wielder to get a good wrap-around hold on the knife in his clenched fist. For thrusting, the blade is punched into the target, while effective slashing can be accomplished either backhand or forehand. Since this type of grip is so strong, it is also difficult to dislodge a push dagger from the hand with a kick, blow or unarmed block.

The "Terminator" from Cold Steel, possibly the best push dagger for self-defense currently available.

Many experts dismiss the value of this weapon for self-defense. They contend push daggers just are not long enough to reach vital organs. If the citizen's goal in carrying a self-defense knife was strictly to KILL, then this criticism would be relevant. But unlike a soldier or assassin, the civilian's goal is simply to stay alive; whether or not an assailant is killed or maimed as a result of your defense is secondary. The double-edged push dagger can slash as well as any knife, and the guy who said it lacks penetration wasn't having one pumped into his chest when he made the remark!

For the trained martial artist, the push dagger can be most valuable. It can easily be incorporated into most hard styles of karate and kung-fu. Because of the perpendicular grip and short blade, back hands, hammer fists, blocks, parries and even clothing or hair grabs can be performed with the knife hand — WITHOUT RELEASING THE PUSH DAGGER. By opening the clenched fist slightly, the knife can be retained between curled fingers while applying heel-of-the-palm strikes. Blows to the side of the neck with the knifehand can be delivered, and a quick raking slash across the throat with the dagger can follow. A wide assortment of hand blows and kicks can be combined with slashes and punching thrusts without substantially changing the basic footwork or body mechanics used in karate and kung-fu. If you can make a fist and keep it closed, you can effectively wield a push dagger.

Because of their size, push daggers can be concealed easily in coat pockets, ready to draw. And since the handle doesn't stick up and the blade is short, you can carry a push dagger inside the waistband of your trousers with-

Because of it's unique grip and application, the push dagger can be retained while executing various types of unarmed technqiues, like the palm strike. It could also be used to block a kick, by slicing across the attacker's shin or calf.

A simple
combination like an
outward block and
slash to the throat
doesn't require much
modification from the
unarmed block-and-
punch sequence
taught in many karate
schools.

For thrusting, the push dagger relies on the basic punching motion prevalent in almost every martial art. Here, an attacker attempts to apply a front choke (1), which results in a quick draw of the push dagger (2) and an immediate thrust to the chest (3).

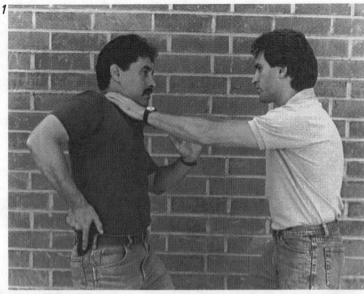

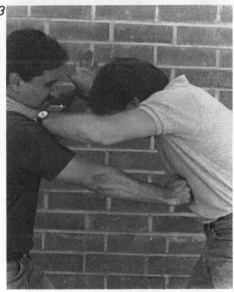

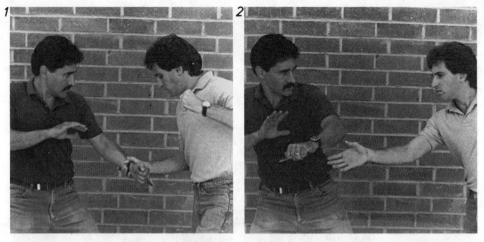

Even a release can be applied while holding a push dagger. Here, an attacker who has dropped his blade attempts to grab the defender's arm (1) but the defender merely jerks toward the thumb to break the hold (2), then uses a backhand slash to the throat (3), immediately followed by a palm smash from the rear hand to end the fight (4).

out attracting much attention, EVEN WITHOUT a coat. One of the most novel designs is the Bowen Buckle Knife, made to resemble a harmless belt buckle.

Instead of trying to learn one foundation of movement for unarmed technique and another for weapons skills, a good case can be made for selecting weapons (like the push dagger) which can be used in conjunction with your empty-hand skills. While the samurai or European knight of old may have needed long-handled and long-bladed weapons to penetrate armor or sever limbs on the battle-field, this is not applicable to the modern civilian or martial arts practitioner.

Most of the best knife targets — throat, eyes, arms, kidneys and chest — can be slashed or stabbed quite easily with a push dagger. Certainly, a knife of this size has less reach than most fighting blades, but this is often a moot point. If you're facing an unarmed man, ANY knife gives you an advantage. If you're facing a gun or stout bludgeon, NO KNIFE gives you an advantage.

The push dagger can provide the civilian with both armed and unarmed capability when attacked in the street. You need not kill or maim unnecessarily, you can deliver unarmed blows while the knife is in hand, ready for any eventuality. You can also react with lethal stabs and flurries of slashes when confronted by multiple attackers or deadly force. Push daggers may not be the ideal self-defense knife for everyone, but they should be considered if you decide to carry a knife for protection.

The Psychological Factor

No matter how you try to approach it, knife fighting is a grisly subject. There is more to it than just the moral qualms involved in taking a life. The true student of knife fighting must harden himself to the brutal nature of life-or-death combat. Blade fighting is a very bloody, messy business. Americans have always been more comfortable with the gun or club; both are relatively "neat" killing tools.

Anyone who seriously considers using the knife in self-defense has got to be prepared to deal with an opponent eyeball-to-eyeball. Fighting with a blade is an up-close, personal affair. You may have to cut or stab an attacker dozens of times to stop him. To do that, you'll need to train yourself to become a knife-wielding savage for a moment in time. If the sight of spurting blood, the entreaties of a wounded attacker or the thrashing and squirming of a man impaled on your blade is going to send you into shock, then DO NOT rely on a knife to protect yourself. Guns are quicker, less personal and much more efficient.

Because fighting with blades is so gruesome, fear is a psychological factor to be dealt with. Being threatened or cut with a knife is a fearful thing, no doubt about it. But fear must be viewed as a POSITIVE emotion in order to condition yourself for combat. Instead of letting your "fear of fear" immobilize you at a critical moment, try to re-evaluate your reaction to it. Think of your fear as a psychological directive that demands a physiological reaction. Although you are not conscious of it, your Adrenal gland begins to provide you with abnormal strength and endurance as soon as fear arouses your nervous system to meet or flee danger. By acknowledging fear as what it is — a valuable biological warning device — you can harness it for the strength you'll need to fight or the endurance you'll need for flight.

One way to turn fear into your ally is to generate moral outrage at your attacker — HOW DARE HE PREY ON YOU OR ANY OTHER PEACEFUL CITIZEN! GET MAD!

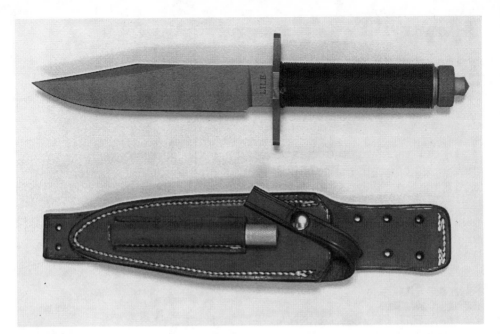

A frightening variation of the Rambo Survival Knife by Jimmy Lile; out on the streets, knife combat is a bloodly, gruesome, eyeball-to-eyeball affair that requires a special emphasis on mental conditioning.

Nothing pushes fear out of the way as well as righteous rage — it can provide you with the sort of "fighting spirit" that will overcome a stronger opponent or frighten off multiple attackers. Once some criminal steps over your imaginary "line" by attacking you, simply UNLEASH on him with everything you've got. Remember, whether you're afraid or not, the attack will occur anyway. Fearing what will happen won't do any good, but taking action, and taking it IMMEDIATELY, may turn the tables. Show your attacker you'll fight tooth and nail, no matter what the odds. Let every cut or wound he may inflict amplify your rage to cancel out the pain, and keep fighting. In boxing, they call this the "killer instinct," and you'll need it to defend your life effectively with a knife.

It isn't realistic to expect that any sort of training will overcome the power of fear, but proper mental conditioning can prevent fear from overpowering you in a time of crisis. Since you cannot banish fear from your mind, you have got to learn to live with it and USE it.

No matter how expensive your knife is, and no matter how well you've been trained, whether you survive or perish will likely depend on whether you've been conditioned to deal with your own emotional reactions to the threat of death. Most people don't deal with such things until the threat of death is upon them. To be a successful knife fighter, you've got to be prepared in advance.

129

How To Treat Knife Wounds

By definition, a person has suffered a wound anytime the skin is opened, punctured or torn. In any encounter with a knife, there is a 90% chance that you will receive at least one cut (most likely more), regardless of your level of skill. For this reason, it is important for you to know how to treat your own — or someone else's — knife wounds.

Minor Cuts

Minor cuts are those which do not result in excessive bleeding and will usually heal quite quickly without professional medical attention. Infection is the primary concern when treating this type of wound.

Most minor cuts will stop bleeding by themselves within 5 minutes; slight pressure on the wound with a clean cloth or bandage may be required to encourage clotting. Once bleeding has stopped, clean the wound carefully with soap and hot water, NOT disinfectants. Iodine, alcohol or merthiolate applied into a wound will damage the flesh and retard healing. After the wound is cleaned, you can apply

For minor cuts or the initial treatment of a wound, raise the injured limb and apply pressure with a cloth or your hand until bleeding subsides.

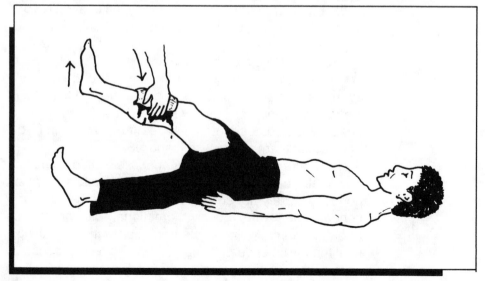

some disinfectant around the outside of the cut and on the dressing to prevent infection during healing.

NEVER close or bandage a wound until it has been cleaned. This usually causes infections. Get all foreign material — dirt, threads, hair — out of the wound by rinsing or with sterilized tweezers. Lift up any flaps of skin and clean beneath them before bandaging. Once cleaned, place a sterile dressing over the cut and tape it into place. Change dressings often while the cut heals.

Some minor cuts may require sutures for proper healing, even though they do not bleed profusely. If the skin on both sides of the cut can be brought together tightly with a bandage, stitches are not necessary. Cuts to the more rounded areas of the anatomy — the cheeks, palm, neck — are almost impossible to close without sutures. If in doubt, seek medical attention after cleaning the cut and applying a dressing.

Serious Knife Cuts

A deep slash or thrust may sever an artery, resulting in serious, fatal bleeding. Here, infection is secondary; if you don't stop or drastically slow the bleeding, you'll be too dead to worry about infection.

There are three basic steps to follow in treating a "bleeder" wound. First, remove, cut or tear away any clothing adjacent to the injury. Next, apply a clean pressure dressing over the wound to encourage clotting, compress bleeding vessels and prevent further contamination of the wound. Hold the dressing firmly in place for 5-15 minutes, until the blood clots. If the wound is to one of the limbs —yours or someone elses — elevate the limb above the heart; this makes the blood flow uphill, and slows it down. After the bleeding subsides, DO NOT remove the dressing! This may tear the clotted blood and bleeding will resume. Tie the dressing in place over the would and get to a doctor. DO NOT try to clean out or close up the wound before stopping the bleeding; deep cuts of this sort will require medical attention, so let them clean the wound in the Emergency Room.

If blood is literally "spurting" out of a wound, then probably a major artery has been cut. Pressure dressings and elevation of the wound will not stop this kind of bleed-

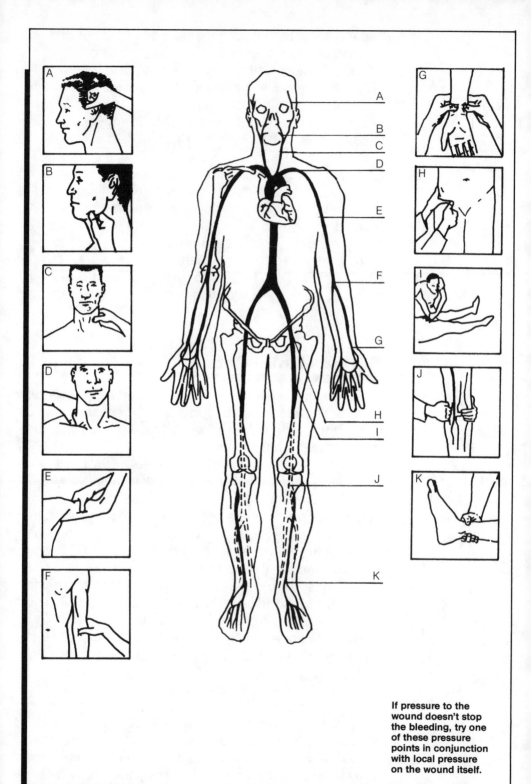

If pressure to the wound doesn't stop the bleeding, try one of these pressure points in conjunction with local pressure on the wound itself.

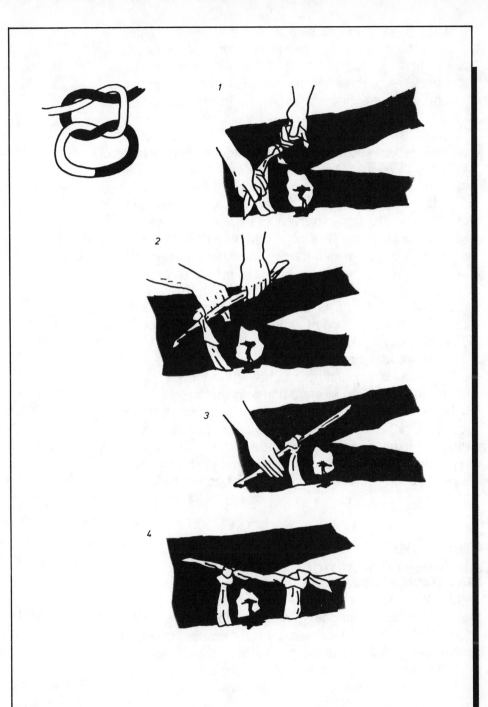

If pressure doesn't work you may need to resort to a tourniquet of some sort.

ing. Using finger pressure, search for the artery about four inches above the wound, between the injury and the heart. You can find it by searching for its pulsation. Apply direct finger pressure to the artery to stop the bleeding.

In many cases, finger pressure will not suffice, and you'll have to use a tourniquet. This is a dangerous LAST RESORT; never apply a tourniquet until you've tried the other steps listed above. Because tourniquets block blood flow through a given limb, the limb can "die" within a matter of hours and require amputation.

To fashion a tourniquet, use a wide belt or piece of clothing broad enough to prevent constriction of the skin. NEVER use rope, wire or thin materials. Wrap the tourniquet around the limb four inches above the wound and slowly tighten the pressure by twisting a stick or pencil slipped through the tourniquet knot. Once blood flow has been controlled, tie the stick into place along the limb with a shoelace or piece of clothing. SEEK IMMEDIATE MEDICAL ATTENTION!

If you are far from the nearest doctor, gently loosen the tourniquet every half hour to see if the bleeding has stopped and to pump some blood into the injured limb. DO NOT release the tourniquet completely; the sudden surge in blood to the limb can result in shock, which is often fatal. If the bleeding has stopped, loosen the tourniquet as much as possible, dress and bandage the wound, and seek help. If bleeding resumes, retighten the tourniquet.

Chest And Abdominal Wounds

Most people who suffer deep penetrating wounds to the chest or abdomen go into shock (a topic we'll cover shortly) and can't be expected to treat their own injuries. If, however, you come upon the victim of a knife attack, the following information may well help you save a life.

Extremely long knives may puncture a lung with a deep thrust, creating a "sucking" wound. This was more common in the days of the rapier and foil, when long blades were weapons of choice. This wound collapses the lung and is virtually impossible to self-treat. If you are

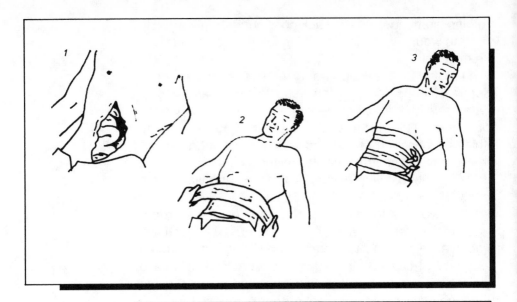

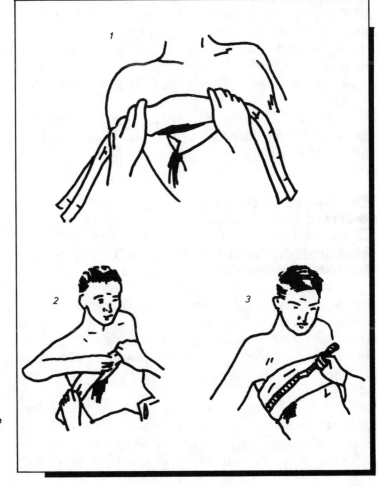

For wounds that expose the internal organs, like the intestines, follow the steps above. For a sucking wound that collapses a lung, follow the steps at right.

treating someone with a sucking wound, you've got to seal the wound with plastic, foil or some other impermeable material.

First, locate the wound and remove any obstructive clothing. If conscious, get the victim to exhale as you seal over the wound, and then tie the seal securely around the torso, trying to keep the seal as airtight as possible. Wrap a blanket, coat or curtain around the torso to increase the pressure on the seal. If possible, get the victim to sit upright. This will help relieve pressure on the lung and diaphragm muscles. SEEK AID IMMEDIATELY.

Stab wounds to the stomach and intestinal area are much more common, and very dangerous. If intenstines, blood vessels or muscle fibers are hanging out of such a "gut" wound, DO NOT try to push them back inside. Leave the exposed organs where they are, and place a clean bandage over them to prevent further contamination. DO NOT give the victim anything to eat or drink since anything swallowed will pass through the severed intestines and spread infection. Leave the victim face-up, head turned to one side, to allow vomiting. If the victim is thirsty, allow them to suck on a wet cloth. NOTHING MORE.

Remember, you cannot control internal bleeding with pressure to the wound, so do not bandage the wound tightly or attempt to apply hand pressure. SEEK HELP IMMEDIATELY.

Death From Shock

The more severe the knife wound, the more likely shock will result. Shock occurs when the body's blood pressure drops extremely low. Loss of blood, organ damage, physical pain and psychological reactions to the sight of one's own injury can all induce shock. This can often result in death, EVEN THOUGH the wound — by itself — is not immediately life-threatening. Signs of impending shock include weak, fast pulse rates, cold sweat and bluing of the face and lips, mental confusion and loss of consciousness.

Whether you have been cut in a knife fight or are attending to someone else, your object is to PREVENT shock from occuring. If you are a trained martial artist or knife fighter, you can probably accept the pain of your wounds without going into shock. Overcoming a revulsion at the sight of your own — or an opponent's — blood is also vital in preventing the advent of psychological shock. This type of Mental Conditioning is essential for the serious knife fighter (as was explained in the previous chapter).

Shock resulting from blood loss, internal injury or excruciating pain is another matter. First stop or control any visible bleeding from the wound. Then elevate the lower limbs, loosen restrictive clothing and apply blankets or warm clothing to prevent chilling. If the victim is conscious, reassure him that you know what you're doing and help is on the way. If unconscious, lay them on one side (head back and tilted low) so that they won't choke on vomit. GET IMMEDIATE AID.

The true knife fighter realizes self-defense training includes more than simply learning how to fight; knowing how to SURVIVE the aftermath of a knife attack is just as important as knowing how to slash and thrust!

Fighting Knives and the Law

Many people rely on knives for personal protection because they dislike firearms. Others resort to bladed weapons because state laws prohibit the carrying of handguns. Almost everyone who carries a knife for self-defense believes it is generally legal to do so, so long as the blade length is less than six inches.

Wrong!!

Most state statutes define a "deadly weapon" as any implement that is, "Used or DESIGNED to be used in a manner which may inflict death or grievous bodily harm." It is clear that this would apply to firearms, but how does a jury or judge determine whether a boot or hunting knife was designed to cut throats or rope? Is a Gerber Mark II designed to saw through saplings or pump into kidneys?

DEADLY BLADES:
"After the Fact"

In most cases, deciding whether or not a knife qualifies as a "deadly weapon" is made after a crime has been committed with it. The judge and jury look to the actions of the knife wielder to determine whether the weapon used might have inflicted death or bodily harm. If a victim has been killed or suffered injuries, the knife is obviously a deadly weapon. Such would also be the case with other makeshift weapons capable of inflicting serious injury: baseball bats, chains, tire irons, etc. The intent of the weapon wielder usually decides the deadly weapon issue. Small pocketknives and even fingernail files have been ruled to be deadly in some states.

While these "after the fact" determinations provide some criteria to a judge and jury in dealing with deadly weapon laws, it is the "before the fact" prohibitions that are of importance to the blade carrier. These prohibitions

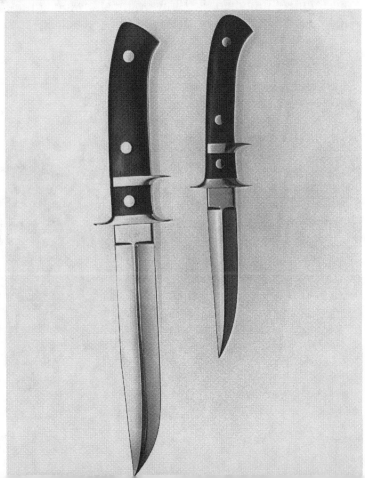

Many people carry folding knives like the finger-grooved Buck Hunter and Ranger models above because they believe such knives are legal to possess. This, however, depends upon what you do with it as well as the vague wording of statutes and local ordinances.

Many statutes prohibit the carrying of any "dirk, dagger or stiletto," without specifying what these knives are. In some states, both of these Crawford knives might be illegal by definition.

assume that certain "tools of crime" are easily recognized and apparent in purpose, and that these items should be illegal for citizens to carry.

DEADLY BLADES: "Before the Fact"

Statutes and ordinances prohibiting the simple POSSESSION of a tool or weapon are known as "strict liability" laws. The possessor's intention (called *"mens rea"* in legal jargon) is not relevant under such a prohibition. Nor does it matter that no criminal act has actually been committed; instrument possession constitutes the crime itself, even if the possessor never USES it. Lock picks, burglar tools, saps, brass knuckles, nunchaku, etc. are considered by many state codes to be instruments of potential criminal activity. Period.

Knives and bladed tools have been around for thousands of years serving a wide range of legitimate uses other than self-defense. So, how do most laws differentiate between those knives used for criminal activity and those designed for legitimate use?

Very poorly.

While strict liability laws that prohibit saps, brass knuckles and lock picks might make sense, how about this ice pick, pen pick or paring knife? In some states, ALL of these have been defined as deadly, prohibited weapons.

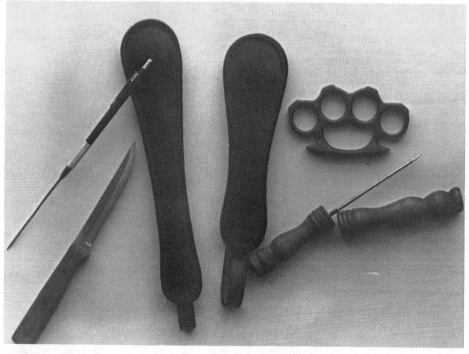

140

Daggers, Dirks, And Stilettos

Simply concealing a bladed tool or weapon cannot be used as a measure of criminal intent, since that would outlaw pocketknives and even nail clippers, (it's hard to think of a Swiss Army knife as an instrument of crime).

Instead, lawmakers over the years have naively resorted to criteria based on unlawful or suspicious "design;" the assumption is that certain knives, BY DESIGN, are made only for killing and/or fighting. Such knives are usually described in the statutes as "dirks, daggers and stilettos." In some states, the Bowie knife is included. Other states — like Colorado — even forbid the carrying of any "dangerous knife or instrument CAPABLE of inflicting cutting, stabbing or tearing wounds." By this definition, even plastic knives and forks might be considered deadly!

In trying to give law enforcement greater leeway and discretion in controlling crime, these laws inadvertantly violate the "Void-For-Vagueness" Doctrine implicit in the due process clause of the 5th and 14th Amendments. This doctrine states that a citizen cannot be held liable for the commission of a crime if the law defines that crime so vaguely that "men of common intelligence must guess at

Which of these Pat Crawford knives are illegal? None of them? All of them? Are they dirks, daggers or stilettos? Does it depend on the blade lengths or the number of edges? It may require a judge and jury to decide!

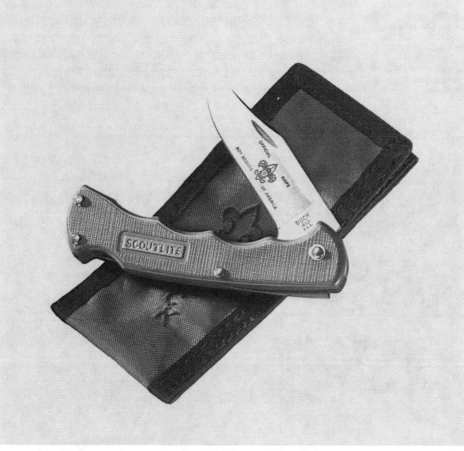

Terzuola,s long,
partially double-edged
fighting knife (top)
might be legal to
carry if worn in
plain sight, but lacking
any precise legal
definition, even the
venerable Boy Scout
Knife might – under
certain circumstances –
be considered a deadly
weapon. Absurd, but
true!

its meaning." But this is exactly what lawyers, judges and juries do in states where the prohibited weapons statutes are extremely broad — they guess! Until such statutes are challenged at the State appeals or Federal level, they will stand as the law, even if they are rarely enforced. *Any person who carries an object that can cut, stab or tear is literally at the mercy of police discretion in many jurisdictions.*

While several states have vague, all-inclusive prohibitions, most states focus on dirks, daggers and stilettos. Problem is, they don't provide definitions for these three knife types. No two dictionaries will provide the same definition for any of the three. They all share design features like "straight-bladed," "double-edged," "symmetrical" and "primarily for stabbing." Sometimes the term dirk is used interchangeably with the term dagger, and a very thin, narrow dagger is often referred to as a stiletto by knife experts. Some states have inexplicably labeled folding "clasp knives" as dirks, prohibiting their concealed carry. Trying to rely on the traditional terminology used by knife enthusiasts has not translated well into courts of law. Without more precise legal definitions of dirk, dagger or stiletto, anyone who carries a Boy Scout knife may be in technical violation of state or local laws.

Some states use blade length definitions for fixed, folding and lockback knives. These states ALSO prohibit dirks, daggers or stilettos, REGARDLESS of blade length, ensuring plenty of confusion. You may not only be arrested for carrying that 10 inch kitchen knife in your coat pocket but also for wearing that small push dagger in plain view on your belt. The first is prohibited due to blade length, the second because it is a dagger.

Stabbing Weapons

Lawmakers have also tried to focus on the stabbing characteristics of knives to determine legality. The assumption is that cutting blades have predominantly legitimate uses —fixing food, cutting rope, carving wood — while knives that stab are intended to kill or injure. This is small solace to the victim slashed to ribbons with a legal knife, and it makes no provisions for awls, icepicks, knitting needles and other legitimate stabbing tools, all of

143

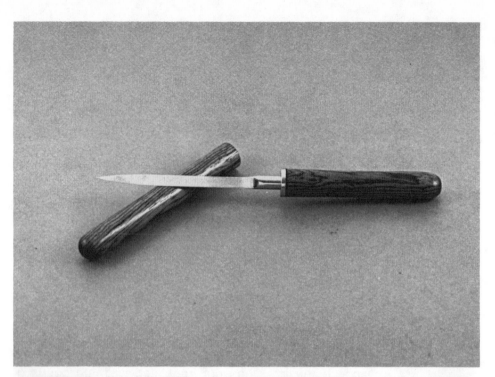

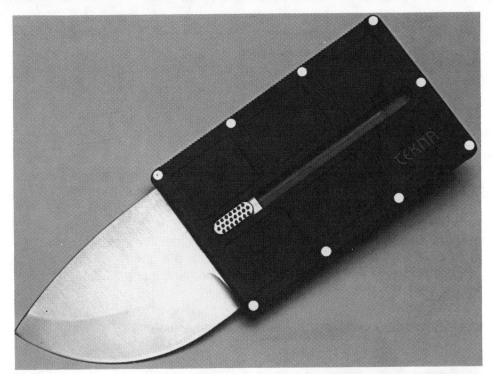

Many statutes use stabbing features to determine whether a knife is a deadly weapon or not. The tri-cornered "Little Sticker" from Pat Crawford (opposite top) would be suspect in many states, but then, so would an ice pick or #16 nail for that matter!

Some states have had the wisdom to exclude hunting knives like these Buck models (opposite bottom) from their deadly weapons statutes. Some jurisdictions, like the Federal Government, rely primarily on blade length to determine legality. This Tekna "Security Card" (above) may have a short single-edged blade, but it's still effective in a pinch as a slashing knife. While this Crawford "Stick Pen" (right) sports a blade under three inches long, its sharpened double edge could be construed as a "dagger design" by a court of law.

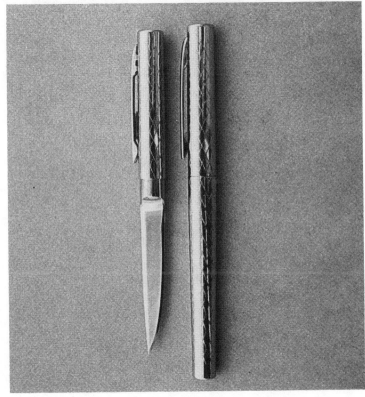

which might qualify as deadly weapons. Nonetheless, the stabbing features of a bladed weapon goes a long way in deciding whether it will be defined as a dirk, dagger or stiletto and thus be prohibited by statute.

In several states, large kitchen knives have been ruled to be daggers EVEN THOUGH only one edge was sharpened. The rationale here is: Since most kitchen knives have such thin blades, both edges needn't be sharpened to facilitate lethal stabbing. Now, if a standard kitchen knife can be considered a prohibited dagger, what can you expect if you're arrested with a fighting knife or even a survival blade? If a prosecutor walks into court with a magazine add describing your knife as a "survival/fighting knife" or as a "push dagger," you will stand a good chance of being convicted. Macho advertising and sales hype CAN be used against you in a court of law.

There are some exceptions to the dirk, dagger and stiletto laws, especially in reference to hunting and camping knives. Certain tools — awls, linoleum knives, razor knives — are specifically excepted in some statutes. But even if your state doesn't legally prohibit your particular blade, city or county ordinances might! Many cities, as well as the Federal government, prohibit a blade length of over three inches in addition to any state laws to which you are already subject. This is known as overlapping jurisdiction, and for the knife carrier, it means confusion galore! Your under-three-inch boot knife may be legal so far as the city is concerned, but the state law prohibiting daggers may still apply! In many states, it is only a misdemeanor to be caught with a concealed handgun, while you can be charged with a felony for possessing a dirk, dagger or stiletto!

Concealment

While many states simply forbid the carry of ANY SORT of dangerous knife, others are more concerned with concealed carry. Determining what is and is not concealed, however, is not all that easy. In Alaska, the statute stipulates that "...a deadly weapon on a person is concealed if it is covered or enclosed in any manner so that an observer cannot determine that it is a weapon without removing it

Many states also prohibit the carry of specific types of knives—or any knife—in a concealed manner. Some states have even ruled that simple folding pocket knives, like the 300 series (top) or heftier 700 series (bottom) from Buck may be construed as deadly weapons if carried in the pocket.

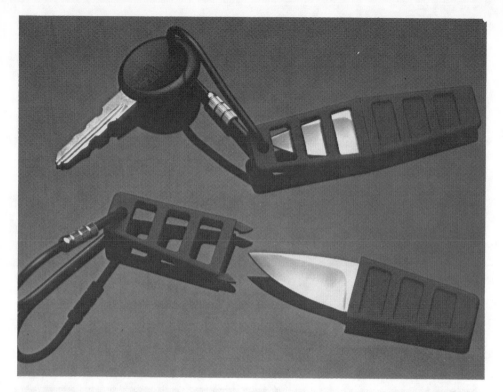

from that which encloses or covers it." Technically, this makes all folder pouches illegal, since they completely cover the knife. And any belt-sheathed knife would become a concealed weapon as soon as you put on a coat. So how to carry a knife on a cold Alaska day? To satisfy this statute, AS WRITTEN, you'd have to keep the knife in hand, in plain view. Not very practical.

The object of such laws is to provide warning to others that you are potentially armed, but how much of the knife itself must be visible is not clear. The Bowen Belt Knife, for instance, is an illegal dirk in California and cannot be worn in public even though most of the knife itself is visible as the belt buckle.

This "Xtra Edge" keychain knife from Tekna features a skeletonized sheath to shield the owner's fingers; does this "conceal" the blade from the view of others? How much of a knife—and which parts—must be visible in order to be considered in "open view" by the law in YOUR state?

Conclusion

It is not my intention to dissuade citizens from carrying knives as self-defense weapons but merely to point out some of the legal implications most people never consider. Most knife laws vary from place to place and are extremely vague by definition. Beware!

There is simply no validity in the assumption that carrying a knife is legal, nor that to do so is less serious than to be caught with an unlicensed, concealed firearm. If you carry a knife, try to get a weapons permit if they're offered in your state or city. If you can carry knives legally, find out from the state Attorney General's office — NOT from law enforcement officers — just what sort of blades are legal to carry. If you can, get a letter from the AG's office; if you are ever harassed or questioned by police about your knife, you can produce the letter from your wallet. This should indicate to the officers that you are simply a citizen carrying a knife for personal protection, not a criminal out cruising for victims.

Some of you may choose to carry a fighting knife for personal protection even though the laws in your locale forbid it. As a student of the law, I would be the last person to encourage others to thoughtlessly disregard deadly weapons statutes. But, as a student of the streets, I also know that it is more important to survive than to be law-abiding. Just remember, you cannot rely on old, word-of-mouth formulas to determine whether your knife — or any other weapon for that matter — is legal to carry or conceal. The last thing you want is to be arrested for felony possession of an illegal weapon; a weapon you were only carrying for self-defense against REAL FELONS!

Knifemaker's Directory

Norman Bardsley Knives, 197 Cottage St., Pawtucket, RI 02860 (401) 725-9132.

Bowen Knife Co., PO Box 590, Blackshear, GA 31516, (912) 449-4794.

Browning Knives, Rt, Morgan, Utah 84050, (801) 876-2711.

Buck Knives, Inc., PO Box 1257, El Cajon, CA 92022, (800) 854-2557.

Cold Steel, Inc., 2128 Knoll Dr., Unid D, Ventura, CA 93003, (805) 656-5191.

Jack W. Crain, Rt. 2, Box 221F, Weatherfod, Texas 76086.

Pat Crawford Knives, 204 N. Center, West Memphis, AK 72301.

Gerber Legendary Blades, 14200 SW 72nd St., Portland, OR 99223 (503) 639-6161.

Jim Hammond Knives, PO Box 486, Arab, AL 35016.

Phill Hartsfield, 13095 Brookhurst St., Garden Grove, CA 92743

Ka-bar Cutlery Inc., 5777 Grant Ave., Cleveland, OH 44105.

Jimmy Lile Handmade Knives, Rt. 6, Box 27, Russellville, AR 72801, (501) 968-2011.

Al Mar Knives, PO Box 1626, Lake Oswego, OR 97034, (503) 635-9229.

Pacific Cutlery, 3039 Rosewell St., Los Angeles, CA 90085 (213) 258-7021.

Robert Parrish Knives, 1922 Spartansburg Hwy., Hendersonville, NC 28739.

Randall-Made Knives, Box 1988, Orlando, FL 32802, (305) 855-8075.

Running River Supply, PO Box 4465, Riverside, RI 02915.

Tekna Design Group, Box 849, Belmont, CA 94002, (415) 592-4070.

Robert Terzuola Knives, Rt. 6, Box 83A, Santa Fe, NM 87501, (505) 472-1002.

Tru-Balance Knife Co., 2155 Tremont Blvd. NW, Grand Rapids, MI, 49504 (616) 453-3679.

About the Author

Robert S. McKay has spent over 18 years studying and teaching martial arts for the street. An active combat handgunner, weightlifter, and author, McKay's defensive techniques have been featured in **Soldier of Fortune, American Survival Guide, Karate Illustrated, Inside Kung-Fu, Official Karate, Combat Handguns, American Handgunner**, and a host of other survival and self-defense oriented publications.

A graduate of the Chapman Academy and a former IPSC Section Coordinator, McKay is currently a law student who teaches a basic three-month self-defense course for St. Martin's College in Lacey, Washington.

UNIQUE LITERARY BOOKS OF THE WORLD

Also publishers of:
Inside Karate
Inside Kung-Fu

UNIQUE PUBLICATIONS
4201 Vanowen Place
Burbank, CA 91505

PLEASE WRITE IN
FOR OUR LATEST CATALOG